VEDANA

VEDANA

The Anguish

Hitesh Sharma

KALPAZ

ISBN: 978-93-5128-024-8

Price: ₹ 250

First Published 2014

Published by

Kalpaz Publications
C-30, Satyawati Nagar,
Delhi - 110052
E-mail: kalpaz@hotmail.com Ph.: 9212142040

Laser Typesetting: Rajender Vashist, Delhi
Printed at: G. Print Process, Delhi

Cataloging in Publication Data--DK
Courtesy: D.K. Agencies (P) Ltd. <docinfo@dkagencies.com>

Sharma, Hitesh.
Vedana = The anguish / Hitesh Sharma.
p. cm.
Novel.
ISBN 9789351280248

1. Religion and politics--India--Faction. 2. Hindus--India--Faction.
3. Muslims--India--Faction. 4. Political faction, Indic (English).
I. Title. II. Title: Anguish.

DDC 823.92 23

Heartfelt thanks to
Pt Saurabh Vashisth

With the blessing of

Acharya Kamal Kishore 'Shivani'

Inspired by–

Dr A P J Abdul Kalam

'O my country's citizens,
Just fill your eyes with tears
And remember those martyrs
Who've died for country's sake.'

Invisible Writer

Pt J P Sharma
29.12.1942 to 06.03.2012

Disclaimer

All characters appearing in this work are fictitious. Any resemblance to real persons, living or dead is purely coincidental.

Hitesh Sharma

Contents

Preface

It was a bolt from the blue for Naved to see his fiduciary love relation become public; not only he but no one ate anything.

Dr Amanullah tossed through the night in anxiety and fear, and very hardly managed to catch on some sleep. Again the same dream flashed through his mind recalling which would always shake his heart and soul. He saw the same old man with open arms, muttering something distressingly........... As if to say "Don't go with them, son........... Please don't go..........Come back..........We are waiting for you........Come back home, son........ Please don't leave your father alone..........Don't fear them........ Don't turn your back to your family."

A series of gruesome scenes followed and began to run in his sleepy mind; one time he saw himself and the old man amidst a huge gathering of Hindu saints and *Sanyasis* rallied together at some Hindu pilgrimage, when suddenly a malicious cavalry of

Arabian assailants brandishing swords and spears raided them and started savagely massacring them.

The other moment he saw hills of the Hindu skulls with the skull-face of the old man lying within.

And then, all of a sudden his uncontrollably racing heart and pounding head threw him out of the dream into reality.

Hitesh Sharma

1

Speech of Truths

"Is it really against the country's law to read, write or speak something about what is actually happening around?

India, a country divided in the name of race and community does not come at a par with its title of being secular, though it has been secular for ages, in the past, any fanatic invader could easily come and own her assets. But in the freedom struggle, people from all races and communities took part with alacrity, put all out efforts, made sacrifices and martyred themselves for geographical liberty. Some communities gained their part and immediately after moments of freedom, the country divided into two in the name of religion. One part became Islamic but the other is still infuriating under the fire of secularism and facing communal frenzies in fits and starts....

Why so?

It is the result of biased and sordid politics, as well as that of ill thinking. The Hindus were liberal with them and the Muslims who did not leave the Hindu dominated part were taken into nobody's consideration and the same with that of the Islamic nation (across the border almost all the Hindus have been compelled to convert to Islam and now the residual are emigrating to Hindusthan). A bunch of selfish politicos divided the country and started ruling their parts respectively. But those people were shrewd enough not to let go of a few Hindus and Muslims to their respective sides only because it was important to run the businesses of their successors. It was a new foundation being laid for an upcoming division, as communal riots are so frequent here where minority suffers; though majority too suffers but that does not count because secularism has to be followed and the meaning of which here is to take care of only the minority. Due to sense of insecurity, people from minority frequently attack majority and in self-defense they do the same thing....

Retaliation goes on and the disturbance caused claims lives of people who indeed are alike in many aspects. Thus, the root cause is communal fanaticism. The rat race for increasing the population of a particular community is also tracking the nation off its course of development.

It is easy that we live together but there is a kind of pungency that keeps us apart. In actuality the Muslims come from the ancestors who were forced to convert to the other faith by the invaders, who wanted to spread their religion, teachings, community and creed. Those ancestors were under great agony which drove them into taking an oath on all their divine holdings to come back home one day, but their progenies forgot the pain of their ancestors and over time have adapted themselves to the change. But it is never too late to start.

Now this country is going to meet its destiny. Everyone knows that history repeats itself but as far as I am concerned there is only one community in this world that does not follow this belief and tries to escape the situation like a pigeon sitting with its eyes closed unknown to the upcoming danger.

It is an irony that the only country of the Hindu community is no longer belonging to it. And they don't even bother to move a straw to save this country. What would happen when the name of this country and religion would only add to the pages of chroniclers' files?

Now coming back to the term secularism—The word 'secular' itself is no less than an abuse, an insult–infidelity. For a country like India that is the birth place of four religions this is not one hundred per cent untrue. Being secular means being infidel and the one who does not follow any belief, religion or faith. This is again one of the greatest ironies that the law makers and the politicos of a country which has always been recognised for its religious, spiritual, cultural wealth and liberation in the whole world, gaily call themselves and love to be called secular. In fact they don't because the term secularism has been imposed upon them forcefully by the state.

Now . . . Why? The politicians of this country are so illiterate, unknowledgeable, indifferent and famished for the 'Millipede-Chair' that they cannot differentiate between secularism and sovereignty.

Mumbai is the only city in the world which has witnessed repeated terrorist attacks. When will the country realise if Mumbai has faced such attacks, the country is no longer safe? Now it is high time for the country to wake up and permanently eliminate the problem of terrorism with her neighbour.

It is obvious that no disease in the world can be cured without a remedy. The task is easy today because it has something in its hands, but in the time to come there will be an army of the terrorists which will be bigger, stronger and better organised than the army of the country itself.

How long will we keep sitting on our hands?

Now let's explore the roots of problem of Pakistan.

After division two divided entities divided their resources and settled things between them. But unfortuitously an issue or two were left unaddressed that never let the two countries become at par. Now who knows these issues were left intentionally by the subtle policy makers or they didn't understand the necessity to resolve them at their infantile stage.

Our neighbour Pakistan shares the same heritage or culture as India does. The difference between lifestyle and mentality etc. between the peoples at large of the two nations is minor.

What is the difference?

People in India are sandwiched between stingy demagogues and the extremists and/or the dividing factors that don't let the nation advance. The situation is the same with regard to Pakistan. Other thing seems being equal they have islamicised army in place of politicians. However the conflict in Pakistan is in the worst condition in comparison to India as a result of which Pakistan has already undergone a division that is called Bangladesh.

Post liberty India has been led by the Congress Party for the most part of time, and so far we have had only one leader who was able to deal with these issues with intention and determination—say Indira Gandhi to name who unfortunately fell victim to the hateful paranoia of fundamentalists.

Or else, all others who succeed the chair only pass time in compromise with the secular muscle or their own dogheaded allies.

Today the country called India is on the verge of becoming a victim to slavery for a second time, but this time to its corrupt politicians and dharma chauvinists. Due to the favour of its neighbour and its own myopic politicians it will break into pieces. The way the major community is being aimed at, their interests being destroyed all over; the day is not far when majority will demand for a new and safe state. The speed at which globalisation of Islamic terrorism is happening forces us to imagine a day when non-Islamic people would be searching for a new planet for them to live. America has got haven on Moon and Mars. Every terrorist attack, be it in the old world or the new world, is found to have included Muslim bigots.

Why?!

Islam, literal meaning of which is brotherhood and fraternity, has been distorted badly by its 'Saviours'- terrorists and extremists. All the names that appear after every terrorist attack are those of Muslims. The Islamic world is observed with an eye of suspicion, then a few liberalists from the

Mohammad maniac community appeal to the whole world that Islam and terrorism do not have any relation, and things become usual once again, but terrorist activities keep on increasing rapidly. This liberalists' action towards the Muslim terrorists does not work, they have to take some hard steps.

Everybody knows Islam has got a fixed line of action, so in the interest of public at large the responsible Muslims should give out the hardest of fatwas, so as to rein in the terrorists and warehouse of militancy. But the ignorance of the Muslims in general causes people to think something beyond.

Why do Muslim preceptors from Deoband, Jama Masjid, and Ajmer and so on, not raise their voice against the only terrorist country in the world-Pakistan, although many Muslims also fall prey to militancy?

Now let's return to what we were talking about, and recollect what had happened on July 26, now you will call it good news or whatever, three men from the Muslim community joined the armed forces of India in different ranks. Their names were Mohammad Shakil, Mohammad Sharif and Abdul. They did it because their religion expected them to or their own hearts guided them so. Now, it wouldn't be good news for a country continuously under threat that people with psychology that of the terrorists from the enemy country intrude its army. But the politicians of this unlucky country do nothing but make face-saving and placating statements and return to their impenetrable 'Buckingham Palaces' in their beaconed and air-conditioned cars with hard chasing entourage of beneficiary insects.

Well, speaking of such things can be precarious too. I would rather expect our country to follow the religious structure along its constitution and keep the world under the sway.

I have no words to describe our country with such an enormous tradition and culture (earlier famously tagged—the Golden Bird and the World's Spiritual Guru). The saga of Arabic-Turkish attacks on India began around fourteen hundred years ago by Mohd Bin Kasim followed by number of successful invaders like Sardar Alaptgeen, Mahmood Gajnavi, Mohd Gori and so on till Aurangzeb. All of them were bruter and crueler than the others. And the same intrusion continues still today. The Black Death of India by Islamic barbarians is perhaps the bloodiest in human history.

I do not think a problem originally fourteen-hundred-year old can be solved hands down. Communal fanaticism nowadays is at its apex; and no police or security can handle the situation. In fact today leading media houses, politicians, specialised officers or whatever is apathetic to reality. Things are so worse that even a small confrontation leads to a communal unrest. It is so abysmal that even if a Hindu child pours Holi colors on some Muslim children, the market becomes closed and the market of grapevines becomes hot. If a Hindu girl marries a Muslim boy, things are fine, but it's vice versa if a Muslim girl gets hitched up with a Hindu boy. Things are serious when fifty seven Hindus are burnt alive in a train as a recrimination further hundreds of Muslims are sent to the abyss of death. The circumstances have become so explosive, and the reason that foreign elements are responsible for all such mishaps, is not valid any more for the reason that the people who indulge in such tussles are also from us. We are just like a pigeon which closes its eyes on arrival of a cat, in the same way; circumstances will get us fallen prey.

In actuality the Moguls attacked our country just to make it Islamic, but their conspiracy was spoiled due to the interference of the Europeans. When the Britons arrived, they knew this country was going to be Islamic as the Hindus were no more against the Islamic suppression and highhandedness, so they simply followed their notorious policy of 'Divide and Rule'. But the Moguls were smart enough they knew they could snatch away the Indian land from the hands of the Hindus but not from the equal rather stronger Europeans. Hindus too made a never-pardonable fiasco by aligning with the eon-old intruders to oust the rather new ones, who were friendly, progressive and religiously in comparison less fanatic 'traders'.

In fact the arrival of the Angrez was no less than a boon for Hindus, but they converted this boon into a boob. They chose thorns over flowers and contaminated their fate which had rather just begun to take a new shape.

However the Muslims united with the Hindus and fought for freedom but their psychology neither changed nor did it end. Until 1947, that is one thousand two hundred and thirty six years after 711 AD they kept nurturing the same air, as it used to be when Islam first entered India. And the result was out, the nation divided into two the very night before it was free. Mohammad Ali Jinnah brought forth the intrinsic psychology of the earlier Muslim rulers and a country, the expansion of which almost touched Europe in the reign of Samrat Samudragupta, once again smashed down.

The country divided in the name of religion, one part of which, in next to no time, acquired its epitome but the larger part is still left into the quicksand of secularism. I don't object being secular in terms of revering other religions, but when you are dividing yourself on the basis of religion and even after division you declare yourself to be secular, is beyond reason. Anyway it's history now and history as we all know is meant to learn lessons. But in this country who bothers to take lessons from the past? I would say that every Indian should first look back to their history and only then move the country towards the path of progress.

Now my dear countrymen, let's come to the term democracy rather say red-beacon-democracy which has made the Prime Minister's chair within the reach of any Tom, Dick and Harry. Have you ever tried to decipher the talisman of this word? ....No, my countrymen, no, this cannot be unscrambled by you because you are not acquainted even with the basic meaning of it. My words can get on the nerves of some, but it is true that democracy means the rule of the public and in order to be successful the demos; that is the public should be uniform and progressive for example like that of Italy, Japan, France and other such countries. We see that in such nations democracy is successful because the public at large is educated, advanced and they are less fragmented on the basis of race, religion, status and language. Do we see such attributes in our country??

Of course not, the things here are just the opposite. A large portion of the society is illiterate, stereotyped and conservative and is badly sectioned on the basis of demographics and other factors. All these phenomena lead to the failure of the democratic structure while in a successful democracy all the citizens contribute to the progress of the country on the whole but in a failed democracy like India, the citizens, lacking in esprit de corps, work only towards their relatively smaller and individual interests rather than the society at large, which nurtures the monster bug of corruption, decaying the country furtively and rampantly. Every instance of scam swipes away motza of public money in a single stroke.

Now see, who is leading the system; the public or a few government contractors who are doing their best in making the public poorer like never before by frequent scams?

The state says that it exercises the right to equality very well but the public is very well not treating one another with equality only because the society is badly broken down into pieces on the bases of the various social and communal paraphernalia. Every larger section wants to dominate or gobble up the interests of smaller sections just like we see in the sea-the big fishes swallowing the smaller ones.

The society is so disappointingly disintegrated that any similarity is almost absent among different segments, feelings of disparity and discrimination are so intense that every smaller class wants their good at the loss of the other. This causes the clash of interests among various groups of the society and this exemplifies the lack of co-ordination among different groups of the society which hinders heavily the success of the democracy where every smaller group tries to dissect itself from its own larger community rather than coordinating with its similar section of the larger society. For instance, a Punjabi while treating a Harijan considers him as a Harijan first and a Hindu or an Indian only later.

Now let's come to literacy and education in India. We all know the status of education in India. A large percentage of population of India is uneducated. As far as I know only sixty-five per cent of our populace is literate but to be very clear there is a huge difference between being literate and being educated. If I can read A B C, I can officially be called literate but not educated because if literacy is sufficient in this sense we should call a computer the greatest scholar; but my brothers, we don't because by only loading huge information, a computer cannot become a scholar, so gentlemen, we may be good at literacy but we lack education.

Education is meant to give character to a person and good education makes good citizens. It's education that brings real edification, equality, fraternity, socio-economical balance, justice and mutual welfare of the society. If you are really learned you will be united and not divided because good education delivers all those ethical and social attributes that are required to raise a successful democracy such as loyalty, integrity and patriotism and above all love for the country beyond any narrow divisions; because only well educated folks can flourish democracy and not the people divided and so called literate.

Gentlemen, be wide-awake and learned about healthy democracy. Do not be puppets in the hands of bloodsucking political muggers. In a country where around half of its people are untaught, what does democracy mean? What will an ignorant man do barring to follow these modern democratic monarchs without coronet?

Get up my countrymen; get up................Kill off the herd instinct...............

Neither a theanthropic incarnation of God will advent to save you up nor these groups of cooks who have all along spoiled the broth. You need one man to lead the nation in one direction-the direction of tremendous progress as this heterogeneous crowd is not going to benefit the nation till it becomes homogenous in not all but in many important aspects and of course well-educated and desegregated."

"One nation, one leader.................................!

One nation, one leader...............................!

....!"

Professor Sharma switched the TV off and exclaimed, "Hey Bhagwan! These oligarchs will do anything to cash in on people's sentiments and to grab the 'Magical Chair', be it changing the history or the geography of the country!"

"Eek! Where do these today's tsars get such banal rhetoric from???"

Suddenly the doorbell rang and he moved to answer the door.

"Namaskar Pandit ji. Come on in . . . Is all well? I am seeing you after a long time. Vedana met me yesterday in the classroom."

Professor Sharma threw a chain of cordial words at Pandit Bholaram.

"In the raj of people like you, things are always fine," replied Pandit ji meekly.

"Oh!!! Pandit ji, you're embarrassing me!"

"Would you please get some water madam and also prepare some sweet lassi for Pandit ji?" asked Professor Sahib his wife Usha, and before he finished, water was there on the table.

Pandit ji and Vedana took water and placed the tumblers back on the table.

"So what makes you arrive here today?" asked Professor Sahib flipping over a page of the newspaper.

"Well, nothing special Professor Sahib, my daughter has just joined BA in your college. So I wish you could help her somehow by teaching her English," Pandit ji requested.

"Oh! Oh! Why not Pandit ji?" replied Professor Sahib putting down his bifocals.

"She can come to me at 4 o'clock in the late arvo. There are several other students from BA first year who come to me, and yes,...........Naved, son of your Dr Amanullah is coming around too in the same batch".

"That's good! Both of the children will be studying together."

"Here you are Professor Sahib, just swig some lassi."

"Oops! Sorry Pandit ji. Ahh, this habit of mine! I am just stuck among professors all day long. Please try this. And you too child......"

They all began to sip lassi.

"Anyway, Pandit ji just tell me why you have named your daughter Vedana, if I am right Vedana means anguish?" asked Professor Sahib taking a sip of lassi.

"Hearing the stories of exploitation, sexploitation, felonious feticide and discrimination, whatever is happening around with women in our society. Now what should it be if not *Vedana*?" explained Pandit ji with a deep breath.

"I concur Pandit ji, you are right. I myself feel sorry over the terrible plight of our society."

They continued for around an hour.

"I'd best leave now; I am leaving my child in your proximity, so please take care of her, and just tell me the time when she comes here and when she leaves."

"Her timing will be 4 to 5 o'clock after college."

"That's fine! I am at home for lunch that time. Anyway Professor Sahib, I would request your permission to leave now as I have to reach the clinic by 5 o'clock and it is already fifteen to five."

"Bhai Pandit ji, madam has cooked very palatable saag. I would like you to................................"

"Please take a pew."

"Thank you, Professor Sahib......... err........ Please don't trouble yourself..... next time sure......"

And Pandit ji left with his daughter.

2

Intelligentsia

Vedana Sharma, the only daughter of Pandit ji, had two younger brothers Nakul and Vakul, studying in ninth and seventh grade respectively. Both of the brothers studied in Rajiv Gandhi Memorial School situated at Shastri Park, Meerut. They duo were good at studies and even looked alike, though they bore a difference of three years. She, being elder one, had the attitude accordingly. She was an embodiment of simplicity, paragon of beauty, and was unaffected by the so called advance girls' type of attitude and life-style, her presence was like a drop of drizzling rain in the scorching heat. She loved to put on salwar-kameez as she was very far away from the feline nature of narcissism. She loved her younger brothers and helped in getting their homework done. She was a responsible home maker and loved her home very much.

Her mother Vimla Sharma, hailing from a good family, continued her decency and simplicity in her new family and always tried her best to make the Sharma family an ideal one.

Vedana'd just got through her intermediate from the Uttar Pradesh Board with sixty nine per cent marks and so she'd easily managed to get admission in a reputed college (The Meerut College) of the city. She was an assiduous student and always did her work with perfection. Though she would get angry at times but it only added to her charm. Moreover she was an amiable girl with all fine feminine traits.

Pandit Bholaram was a benevolent person with pleasing personality. He was in his late forties and was an egalitarian and philanthropist, and was available to anyone in their hardships. His father Pandit Ishwar Dayal Sharma had spent seven years of life behind bars. He was a freedom fighter and the same virtue had entered Bholaram's genes too. It was in his disposition to work with dedication and trust God upon its outcome. Accepting anything with good grace reflected stoicism in his personality. He worked as a compounder for Dr Amanullah 'VANDE MATARAM' at his clinic; he was there for a long time. His salary, twelve to twelve and a half thousand, was almost sufficient. Though he was an underpaid worker, yet everything was happening for him by His grace. He did his work with his whole heart, and working for so many years had made him so perfect that he even attended to patients in the absence of Dr Aman and moreover all the patients of the doctor were familiar with him.

Doctor Sahib, a social figure and an august personality, was also an editor of a weekly magazine namely 'VANDE MATARAM'. That's why 'VANDE MATARAM' was attached to his name. He had not only made rapid strides as a leading family physician but had also earned a name for himself as a figure against terrorism. He had been heading an Anti-Terrorism organisation 'VANDE MATARAM', and had played pivotal role in the hanging of many Pakistani militants and some Indians too withstanding all the pressure from the mullahs. He was a patriot from the core of his heart. He had three daughters and a son named Naved, the one who studied with Vedana in her class. Naved wanted to appear in civil services examination, so Doctor Sahib helped him fulfil his dream and let him study Arts rather than push him towards Medicine. He had two daughters elder to Naved. They were married, while the third one, Sabiha, was the youngest among the siblings and was a student of twelfth standard in a convent school of repute in the city. She had topped her school in class tenth. She was an introvert and less garrulous girl, and had a good friend Rajiv Verma in class who was the son of a famed dentist in the city Dr Chander Kumar Verma.

With the passage of time Sabiha and Rajeev both grew up. After completing their twelfth Rajeev took admission in Agra Dental College and Sabiha pursued her MBBS in Ghaziabad. Though Rajeev and Sabiha were far apart and their courses were also different, but their childhood friendship continued to bloom. Distance had deepened their intimacy so much that they had talks daily. They'd never shared their feeling to each other; but had become a wont for each other. They revered each other a lot. Both of them were intelligent also.

Right from class one, Rajeev used to come first in class and Sabiha either second or third. Rajeev never came down from his first position. Even in school days, the chemistry between them was a subject of big interest. Their performance was so good that no educator had any problem about their relationship rather this cute link-up was liked by all. Even their male classmates, instead of acting green-eyed, relished their camaraderie. Sabiha got respect from all due to her friendship with Rajeev.

Even some teachers were also aware about this but their demeanour was so refined that they never let their teachers complain against them. They were having a whale of a time; between and around them everything was happening so good that they did not realise how time had passed out.

Khatun Jahan, begum of Dr Aman was a domestic woman and spent most of her time in routine chores, and like any typical house-wife was used to cooking, washing, sewing etc.

Naved a vicenary Mills and Boon hero was a good specimen of eye-catching physique and looked genteel in nature which he was indeed, he minded his own business. He did not make his voice heard and kept himself to himself. He had only one friend named Taufique who thought himself to be over smart and abler but was of a sour mind indeed. Both of them were poles apart by nature. He, more's the pity, was a classmate of Naved and Vedana at Meerut College.

3

Rapprochement

Naved and Vedana were not close friends, they only had developed a kind of affinity as they had been studying together since childhood and also visited each others' house at times in case it required. They duo had been classmates and since they had family relations as well, the closeness between the two had grown overtime, and now they had also started going for tuition together. Naved was calm and composed boy, and Vedana had similar nature and therefore liked people of the same attributes.

She felt attracted towards him, she liked to talk to him, but he was ignorant about how she felt and was busy with his studies and other engagements. Though she had all aspects of beauty, her hair long, black and bushy, her big eyes looking down, her ever-blushing rosy cheeks, her fair complexion, her cuddly physique, only added to her pulchritude profile. When she walked rhythmically, her braid moved to and fro hitting against her hips and when she moved her eyes looking down up, seemed as if an archetype of beauty was being presented. She was so beautiful and filled with freshness but her soberness kept her beauty undercover.

Naved was too shy to speak to girls and kept his eyes down while talking to them. While his friend Taufique was the vice versa, he often said to Naved sanctimoniously,

"Yaar, Vedana talks to you much too. Why don't you get the young woman? She is Hindu and you will be entitled to huge *Shabab* (divine applause), and for this pious act, there is no dearth of money, *Maulvis* and mosques shall help you financially as this is the part of Jihad to take Non-Muslim girls into Islam. If she had talked to me like that I'd have proposed to her for marriage, but the problem is that she doesn't even look at me though she always catches my eye."

Naved, irritated over this, asked him, "Where do you collate all these nauseating things from?"

"Who is there to tell me, you believe it or not, it is true. I like Vedana and I am going to propose to her all in good time."

"Do whatever you want to, but just don't bother me and let me do my work, I want to become an

IAS official," said Naved to the hobbledehoy bringing his palms together.

Taufique left from there and Naved too took his way home. By that time the college had got closed with a few peons around.

That day Naved did not go for the tuition and Vedana missed him. She asked Taufique why Naved had not come, though she didn't like talking to him.

He grinned and replied, "We were just there at college, I don't know what happened to him? He left for his home at elevenish. He did tell me that he'd come here."

"Okay," said Vedana closing the discussion as she didn't want to fall into conversation with him, but she felt compelled. Anyway the tuition got over and she left to go home and busied herself in everyday errands.

That night Naved saw Vedana in his dream for the first time. He got up suddenly and his mind got stuck. The following morning he wondered about what he saw in his dream last night. It was Vedana's face that was hovering about in his eyes, and Taufique's raillery in his ears:

"I'm going to propose to her."

....

"I'm going to propose to her."

....

Next day Naved was not the same guy. He felt kind of void sans Vedana around, something was pulling him towards her. He put on his blue jeans and cream color tee shirt and reached college. As soon as he reached there his eyes began to search for her from everywhere to everywhere and suddenly his eyes paused at a place opposite the IGNOU office in college precinct where she was drinking water, leaning a bit over. As soon as he saw her, he had his eyes stuck on her, looking at her womanly beauty like he had never noticed before and as she turned around, her wet red lips, rosy cheeks, her large and slanting eyes looked as if they were augmenting her comeliness and helping Shakespeare collect material to create an outstanding beauty-sonnet. He quickly headed towards her though he did not know what he would say but all he said was,

"Hi, how are you Vedana?"

"O, hi Naved! I am fine," said Vedana, maintaining herself.

"How are you, Naved?............. Why didn't you come for tuition yesterday?" continued she.

"Well, I was busy at home yesterday."

"With something important?"

"Not so much! I was engaged in making bandobasts for uncle's hadj."

"Achcha, your uncle is going on a pilgrimage to Mecca."

"Yeah, what did sir teach yesterday?"

"Well, we read the poem 'The Flea', a very fascinating poem by John Donne, he is a great love poet and you missed that."

"Ooh, now how'd I do that?...................... Ah, can you give me some idea about that?"

"Yup sure, why not?"

It was 11 o'clock and their class had to start at 11:30, so in the meantime they moved towards staircase leading to the terrace between the Physics and the Chemistry laboratories. The stairs were narrow as the roof was empty and unused, and one stair couldn't accommodate both of them so they sat on single stair up and down.

She started connoting him 'how in the poem 'The Flea', the poet doesn't hit the flea only because the flea has sucked the blood of his beloved before it bit him. He looks at the flea with affection and thinks it's not mere a flea but a union of the two, the poet and his beloved. Though he can't meet his beloved or even touch her, the flea has united them by biting and sucking the blood of both.'

Meanwhile Naved was also trying to touch Vedana somehow and wanted to come closer to her so as to feel her feminine-fragrance. And in this way half an hour elapsed and the couple went off to their class.

Now he started feeling kind of attachment for her. He was being pulled towards her and so he set about getting close to her, talking to her heart to heart and even touching her, though he chattered less.

Taufique on the other hand was rejoiced to see them both coming close to each other as he was their common friend though his being happy was laced with queerness as he was of a peculiar temperament. He harbored in his mind.

"It's good a 'Saffron' girl is coming closer to a 'Green' boy."

He encouraged Naved to become intimate with Vedana, and delivered good and bad stuff about girls and frequently said to Naved,

"Marrying Hindu fair sex is an act of *Shabab,* though it's an uphill task."

Naved didn't think that far.

He'd say to Naved, "How great it would be if every Muslim boy intermarries a Hindu ingénue. Hindu or kafirs then soon will be outnumbered and this country would be called Mugalistan rather than Hindusthan."

He emphasised this country had been made, decked and beautified by their ancestors and that the Taj Mahal, the Red Fort, the Old Fort, the Qutubminarate, the Jama Masjid, the Buland Darvaja, the Char Minarate, the Grand Trunk Road (from Wagah to Kolkata, including the national highways 1, 2 and 91) and other buildings, the glory of the country, had been erected by their forefathers for only them, which now had slipped into the hands of these kafirs.

"This country was ours, it is now ours and will always be, these kafirs will have to leave this country sooner or later and this is a good way to ruin them that we get their lassies and convert them to our faith. This is the only way they will numerically come down. You know Naved! Plus-minus five Hindu girls daily get knotted with Muslim boys in our fatherland, and that too at their own will."

All this bullshit drove Naved crazy and he in turn drove gormless Taufique off in anger. Naved disliked him only because of this trash-talk and since he knew his nature so he preferred to keep his lips static. Naved wasn't so narrow-minded and didn't discriminate between an 'East Conscious' and a 'Qibla Conscious', moreover he believed that everyone has the same origin as well as the same destination. Every person worships the same power with various names and ways. He disapproved of things that disseminated malevolence.

As time went by, Naved and Vedana neared each other.

On 23 December, there was a function at Doctor Sahib's residence. It was the marriage of his elder brother Hadji Sadiqullah's daughter. Pandit ji was invited too with family but only Vedana accompanied him at the function. In the party Vedana primped a white colour star-studded vesture and in that posh apparel she looked like the moon in its full glow among stars though Naved too was not behind anyone sartorially. As he looked at her he could not take his eyes off her, he stared at her furtively but they didn't speak to each other. Pandit ji soon returned home from the midwinter party.

On the other hand Professor Sharma was promoted to the position of Principal by the University Grant Commission and therefore had to be transferred to another city so Vedana had to discontinue her tuition. Now she was in BA final year and since she'd scored good marks in previous years, she no more needed tuition. Now Vedana and Naved did not meet each other at the tuition centre.

After tuition was over, they resorted to meeting at the public parks in the name of studies and later on they switched to meeting at eateries and that's how they started going steady.

She often asked him if it was right but he, being a sook, said, "I too dislike meeting you this way. The Shivasena and the Bajrangdal people are raiding restaurants these days and if we are caught someday, they wouldn't let me off, all the more so because I am Muslim and you, a Hindu."

As soon as she heard him saying such things, she would place her hand on his mouth, "Please hold what you're saying, no one is going to say anything to you."

The couple dated frequently. Overtime they finished their graduation.

It was the evening of 6 January, the disputed erection of Sabri Masjid was demolished and the flames of communal riots consumed the whole country.

A boy in his twenties came running to the clinic of Dr Aman and recounted pantingly.

"*Mamujaan*, shut the clinic, the Hindus have destroyed Sabri Masjid and as a result the riots are spreading all over the city. Our house has been sabotaged too, wherever they're finding our homes in their areas, they're setting it on fire."

"Arey Pandit ji, you're still standing here, just shutter down, run and get home quickly, people are on an onslaught. Bablu, a Hindu friend of mine has just been butchered by the *Ghosies* (Muslims engaged in the business of milk) in their house and things are really awful outside. The markets are all closed down; people are thirsty for each other's blood." Akram, a neighbor, gave an account from the horse's mouth.

"Ugh! Ya Alah, I'll just go home and see whether Hindus are still there," the boy continued moving.

Thus recrimination created blood-brooks.

It's an irony that we humans, created by the power above Allah or Bhagwan and sent by Him to this world for doing creative acts, have divided ourselves somatically in His name, Who is impartial and one when creates us.

The reaction or the resilience of the act rippled through the boundaries of the nation and for the neighbouring country it was a moment they had been waiting for long. As the news flew across the boundary of the state, the people of the neighbouring nation reacted. They set out sabotaging the sancta of the minority of their country; exempli gratia the Rudra Mandir was one among many. So there were reactions all over the world.

Two belligerent communities within a country were fighting as if at war on the international borders. As the situation was carried on, the administration declared emergency and imposed curfew in the sensitive areas and therefore people got statued wherever they were. The scene created after the silence of the curfew was such that could freak out the heart of the stoniest man.

Though we have not seen it but we have heard that our country was titled the Golden Bird and invaders from far deprived it of all its wealth and glory and that they dug out things even from wall. It was just as a butcher does with a chicken by removing all its waste wings and parts. In the same way our motherland had been notched at as well. It is agonising to know that we have always been plundered like this, and the peoples, who did it, tangibly were from outside India who spirited down the country and left the virus of conversion within it and so forth corrupted its system.

The scenario is different now. Their stream of thought, although being centuries old, is still nurturing within their cardio-confines.

Some reporters from the neighbourhood even testified that the minorities and their interests were at danger in India, for which the government had to answer to the whole world.

Such cross-border media terrorism had always very apparently, avidly and strongly been condemned by Dr Amanullah through his weekly 'VANDE MATARAM' and together with invariably admonished Pakistan in printed word for propagating against India.

And here in India a kind of inferior feeling has made the majority Hindus a bit aggressive and now what they feel is that, this country is called Hindusthan, the world knows it, and it has been divided in the name of Hindu and Muslim even then.............! More cardinally Ajodhya is significant for Hindus in the same way as Mecca and Medina are for Muslims and The Vatican City is for Christians. It is because Lord Ram took birth here and yet other groups, instead of helping, are giving value to a *Makbara* constructed by a terrorist. Due to these reasons, the chasm between the two communities has been widening.

Anyway, Vedana started preparing for her BEd entrance test after completing graduation and applied for this course in different universities and cleared her BEd entrance test at the second attempt from Kanpur University. She took admission there and shifted to Kanpur for one year where she stayed at a hostel.

On the other hand Naved took admission in MA English. Although he was an above average student, yet he failed to secure good marks in his first year, but he worked harder and was sure to get 75 per cent in the second year. He along with joined for a few months coaching classes for Civil Services entrance examination and at times went to his father's clinic too.

One day Professor S.K. Gupta, a good friend of Dr Aman, came to his clinic. In course of talks Professor Gupta inquired about Naved and Dr Sahib apprised him that he was doing his MA in English and that since November he had been attending preparation classes for the Civil Services too.

"What option do you plan for him? There are so many prospects after an MA in English. Send him to me and I'll prepare him further," suggested Professor Gupta.

"Do you understand, Naved? Professor Sahib is calling you, just go and meet him in the evening as he has got some plans for you," said Dr Aman.

"Sure dad, I'll be there."

In the evening while going to Professor Gupta's bhavan, Naved's phone rang,

"Naved................"

"Vedana......... Where are you calling from?"

"Meerut................."

"When did you come?"

Vedana'd just opened her mouth to speak when Naved interrupted.

"It's just been 10-15 minutes. You know what date is today?"

"Yeah... It's the fourteenth. Oh, Oh! You're so rough and candid. It is February fourteen today. It's Valentine's Day!"

"Ohh... I see, Valentine's Day, so dear, what's the mood?"

"Would you like to be my valentine?" he continued.

"I don't know what you mean. Don't you have the same mood or something? You reach there at *Sheetal Grand* shortly and I will also get there as quickly as flash after getting fresh."

"And if you're behind time or don't reach........?"

"No dear, think as if I'm virtually there! In fact I am on my way to Professor Gupta's house. I'm very near to the *Sheetal Grand*. Now just put phone down and get there.............."

"Hurry up!"

"OK dear, Bye!"

And they had their plan for 14 February. Soon she reached there.

After joining BEd, she had become a little more sophisticated.

She gussied a pink salwar-suit with a sky blue jumper over it and looked eye-catching in her dress. She was already genetically beautiful but that day she looked no less than a nymphet.

Both of them reached the first floor. The restaurant had special arrangements for Valentine's Day. There were lovey dovey couples all around indulged within themselves and looked like two bodies with one heart and soul. She nudged him in the elbow romantically to take a corner love seat, they sat and ordered vanilla fudge with espresso and became one among the others and commenced floating in the ocean of love. Everyone had gifts for each other. All were so much imbibed in loving words that they had even forgotten about the coffee and snacks they had ordered that they were getting off.

Romantic songs playing in the background were making the air in the restaurant more appealing.

"Tchah! This old fuck is spoiling the atmosphere of the city, finish off his bistro today..................."

"Some of you go up there and the rest would hand out *rakhis*, get them to do hundred sit-ups each."

"Call their parents; take the phone numbers from them."

Suddenly, a hail of shouts rocked the eatery. There were sounds of boom and bang coming from down there and within seconds the love-sleep of all the couples sitting there got vanished. Many of them didn't take time to understand that was the moral army of the Shivasena and the Bajrangdal, so they made way to scatter away. It all came about so suddenly that they failed to think how to respond, some of them mingled with those hoodlums and started shouting *Jai Shree Ram*, *Har Har Mahadev* et cetera, so as to shun insult before their girlfriends.

Around two hundred to two fifty men were there in and outside the restaurant; they were all armed and were all shouting *Jai Shree Ram* and slogans like this. The behaviour of the gang of roughs was very uncivil; many of those hoons behaved sassily with girls, frisked them nastily and threw hands at their bags and other belongings. There was hullabaloo all around. At the protest of the girls, a few seniors among them came forward to help them out and started asking them their names, addresses and phone numbers, Vedana too was inquired. They asked who she'd come with.

Seeing this Naved jostled his way out of the crowd and cried.

"You have misunderstood brother; she's doing her BEd from Kanpur and has only arrived today. We were just sitting here and sharing pleasantries."

"*Abey oye*! Just tell us your name and we'll call someone from your home too," bellowed one from the throng.

"Brother, I'm son of Dr Amanullah," said Naved shivering in fear.

"Yecch! Get that bastard fella. He's a Muslim," and so around ten to twelve boys broke upon him.

"You did not find a Hindu guy? Choose one, we are many here," hollered one of the yobs inanely.

At this point some gray leaders objected and rebuked the rude skollies.

They stopped teasing Vedana and hitting Naved. The police arrived on getting an anonymous phone call; seeing the khaki clad men, a number of them became volatile, while the other senior group members surrendered themselves to the sheriffs shouting so-called religious slogans. This way the matter almost finished. The police sent the lasses to their addresses and took the lads along with them in their jeeps.

It was all so despicable and shocking for Vedana, she was shivering in fear. She controlled herself somehow and went straight to her friend Srishti.

She was so frightened; she splashed her face with cold water and endeavoured to come out of the dark valley of the shock. She took her time then she set out for her house. By the time she reached there, she seemed normal from the outside, but unsound reveries of the recent happenings were whirling around within her mind. She was much worried about Naved so she was unable to set her mind on anything at home and she continuously tried his cell phone.

There Dr Aman received a call from the police station. He was asked to come there and take his son on bail who had been convicted of causing social disturbance. He reached the police station perplexed. He took an account of whatever had happened and bailed out his son. Cops at the police station informed him how his son was caught at a bistro with several girls. At the police station he nodded along with the cops but on his way back home he asked Naved the truth.

Though he trusted Naved, he was interested in what had actually happened. Naved was an honest and straight-forward boy, so he made no bones about telling his father everything forsooth. By the time he finished his account, his father was unable to feel the ground as he didn't want to brush along with any controversy. He realised immediately that his son had grown up and hade gone off the trail."

"She's Hindu, son, you shouldn't move any further," dissuaded Doctor Sahib.

"Things have already advanced, dad, there's no issue about being Hindu or Muslim now," clarified Naved easily.

"Are you thinking of marrying her?" interrupted Doctor Sahib.

"Yes, and you will get the same answer if you ask Vedana, dad," asserted Naved.

"*Lahaul Vilakuwwat*! You naïve children! What are you into? The society will never accept this and here we will be facing wrath from both the sides."

"Didn't you hear about the case of Laxmi in the news? A Hindu girl from Modinagar, who ran away with a Muslim boy and married him, the boy was slain by Hindu extremists. The couple was being forwarded to the judge and the court was packed and ad interim some men, must be hit squads attacked them suddenly and burnt them alive." Doctor Sahib raked up a bitter episode to cast out the evil spirit of love from his son.

Naved didn't stop himself, "Dad! You're with us. Just help us."

Doctor Sahib nodded just to keep the heart of his child but a profound fear penetrated his heart at a stretch. Anyway they got home talking so and so. It was calm there and things were normal but his mom got surprised as she saw them both at the clinic's timing. It was eight while Doctor Sahib normally came back home from the clinic at about 10 O'clock. He had left clinic under Pandit ji.

She surprisingly enquired, "How come you're back so early today?"

"I just took Naved to Professor Gupta," Doctor Sahib prevaricated.

"Give me some water, I'll leave for the clinic now and will be back early today so be prepared with the dinner."

"Yeah, I'll cook dal, bhindi with paratha. If you wish something else, tell me, I'll do timely."

"No it's enough; remember salad of mooli and cucumber with the dressing."

"Achcha," she said in reply.

Doctor Sahib came back home early, nibbled his dinner and went straight away to the bedroom. At night he saw a dream.

4

The Trance

"There's a desert like place where there is a big temple. The gale is blowing strongly and sand particles with withered leaves seem as if ghaists are dancing in front of an idol of Lord Shiva. The sandstorm is blocking the people's view but what he sees through is that some people are trying to smash down the temple. There are around 2000 to 2500 people gathered for worship; but they all are standing in a queue with their back towards the shrine. The sun's shining hard. Some horribly large birds are hovering around, making fierce noises as if signaling something horrid was going to come about. Suddenly he sees a troop of horses advancing at a gallop towards the temple. A man with long and black beard is pioneering the troop. He moves forward and stops in front of the queue of the people and roars something acrid. He gets down from the horse and moves through the rising clouds of dust.

When he reaches the people, they see him holding a thick book in one hand and a luminous sword in another.

The beardie brandishes his sword in the air and vociferates,

"Be all ears and eyes, you're given two choices—there is Quran in my one hand and a sword in the other. You have to choose one."

"Decapitation or Islamisation; the choice is yours."

His words instil fear and anger among the mob but they don't have any other option but to give in to this sacrilege, so one by one they reluctantly raise their hands for the Quran. But there is an old man who breaks at the last moment and instead of giving in to that bestial man's desire, likes to be beheaded audaciously. On seeing this the man next in line breaks into tears with acute pain. He screeches helplessly.

"Why did you slay my brother, Aurangzeb, why?"

"What wrong did we Hindus do to you?"

"Who will look after his children?"

He breaks down and accepts the proposal weeping and wailing. He takes his brother's lifeless body home in his arms and cremates the corpse in the courtyard of the house and erects an almirahtemple in his memory on it in order to keep the next progeny abreast of the Islamic repression. Below this structure he buries all things of religious significance (idols of Gods and Goddesses and others).

The sinister saboteurs of Aurangzeb visit each house everyday to make it sure that all villagers relinquish worshipping the idols and start following Islam. In whichever house they find people stuck to their old religion (Sanatan), they rape all the women and murder all the men.

When it is turn for Doctor Sahib, he falls back and the moment he does so, the sword shines to dissect his head in a single blow. Suddenly out of heaven a divine streak of light passes through and takes Amanullah away from Aurangzeb. Amanullah sees the face of that slain old man in that streak of light."

They are still being followed by the sword of him.

And the next moment Doctor Sahib popped out of the nasty dream, he woke up flurriedly dripping in perspiration, sweating and shivering in fear. He slept alone in his room and moreover it being small hours, no one came to know about his dream but he never forgot that dream.

The next day there was heartbreaking news in the air; serial bomb blasts had rocked thirteen different cities across India. It was as if terrorists had set in a war against the country. Place to place, bomb blasts and plethora of victims like road-kills were around and only two voices were being aired in the milieu, one from the bullets of terrorists and the other of the people screeching who'd lost their dear ones.

It was the dark day of 15 February, when bullets of terror pierced the bosom of the nation. It seemed as if terrorists were hidden in each lane and street of the country. The Prime Minister had come back from his Dhaka visit to Delhi in a hurry to take charge of the situation; blasts were still taking place over and over at one point or the other sporadically. Never had ever happened that ere?

Earlier bomb blasts would occur in a city or two once or twice but this time the instance of bomb blasts simultaneously in a number of big cities was aimed at toppling the whole country down rather than making it local or regional news.

In Lutian's Delhi, North Block witnessed back to back high level meetings and the Home Minister Mr Salman got completely dumbfounded when came across the media.

On the contrary Indian media covered that tragedy too in its well-known and patriotic 'cover-all' way. By 3 o'clock there were ten in capital and equal number of blasts had jolted other cities; in the wake of which there was pandemonium and stampede all around. All of a sudden Defense and Home affairs were put on alert. The headlines pertaining to encounters between police and terrorists were on air and news of blooding, murdering and looting too began to be flashed.

At the Prime Minister's house a high level meeting on this arduous situation, attended by the leaders of all national parties, ended up with a decision that media should be restrained and all cities of importance must be handed over to the army. At four in the morning, a proclamation passed and the media was advised to cover and video fully but it could not telecast it the same way; and the army was also commanded to come out of the cantonments. By 4:30 a.m. all the Metro cities of the country were in the hands of the army. Article 144 was enforced in all the cities and for the next two and a half hours the army and terrorists clashed fatally in various cities.

Though media was not ordered to televise the encounter, yet they could air the news without any video clipping. By 7 o'clock in the morning, news of war came down. There was gloomy ambience all around the country and the public was stunned. It stirred the nation deeply.

In next two days, things started normalising.

After investigation a new nexus came into light, consisting of the lady officers on espionage of the

Inter Services Intelligence, the Federal Bureau of Investigation agents and the sleeper cell of the Indian *Muzahidin* and a few other regional terrorist groups. In the pockets of some dead terrorists, small poly pouches were found containing a white powder about which government never disclosed anything. As a product of these attacks chaos prevailed everywhere that took a colossal toll on the communal harmony. Riots began between two major communities and consequently lotta innocent people were burnt alive in frenzy.

The fire of hatred reached the college of Naved's sister also.

She was doing MBBS from a college of Ghaziabad and when the news came, she was in class.

A peon rushed to the class and informed the lecturer gaspingly,

"Sir, city is burning in communal antagonism and people are slaughtering one another."

The lecturer abruptly discontinued the class and advised the sophomores to go back to their respective hostels. The main gate was closed on the principal's fiat. Sabiha too advanced to the hostel.

Doctor Sahib planned to go to Ghaziabad to bring Sabiha back home but it was a tall order, as curfew was in force in most of the cities, so he kept in touch with the principal on-line till the situation eased off.

The politicians got hold of the wrong end of the stick and failed to simmer down the fire of hatred; therefore army took up the job and mollified the country within the next five days.

Vedana there had good kismet as after just a general investigation she was sent home by the police and riots let the police keep this petty issue aside and so at her home nobody ever knew what had happened. The next morning what she did first was phone Naved.

They exchanged the aftermath of the unpleasant event with each other and she was stunned to learn that he had told his father everything. She mummered nervously,

"Get an oath from your dad that he won't tell anything to my dad." She tried to figure him out.

"Does anyone know anything at your home?"

"No"

"Oh! *Shukr-E-Alah*! Sure! I'll explain everything to my dad; in fact he is in worrit about Sabiha as she is still at the hostel and yes, I don't believe in oaths and all that."

"Again, do you know what do?"

She disconnected the phone in the middle having heard some foot steps approaching her.

Well, altruistic Doctor Sahib was himself wide awake so he didn't disclose anything to Pandit ji. Since it wasn't a trivial matter and she was like daughter to him, so he thought it better to conceal things.

On 21 February, Vedana went back to the hostel but now she didn't want to stay at the hostel any more. And being under a lucky star she came to know that the same Professor Sharma who had taught her in her BA was the new principal of her college and she informed her dad about that with great felicity.

"Dad, there are girls who are regular but will appear for examination on term-end only. You please speak to Professor Sharma and get the same kind of arrangement for me too."

"Is it?"

"Sure dad, if you wish I'll make you talk to the girls who are given this facility."

"It's OK, but I don't have his contact number, you just go get it, I'll talk to him."

Vedana did that.

Pandit ji spoke to Professor Sharma in this regard and Vedana's fa' favoured.

And she came back to Meerut. Now she was a non-attendant student and was preparing for exams at home only.

5

Jihad and Love

One day Naved met his old friend Taufique, in passing he told him how Hindu hardliners attacked them when he had gone to meet Vedana, and how he had been thrashed only because of him being Muslim.

"You're doing pretty good for Islam that you've snared a tilak-wearer girl; now be quick and do jihad," emitted bigheaded Taufique. Naved knew jihad but he couldn't figure what his friend meant.

"What do you mean by jihad?" he asked the rotted minded.

"Jihad means *Islam ki Dawat* (invitation to Islam), when you do jihad, you invite people to adopt Islam or anyhow convert kafirs to Islam. Walk down the aisle with Vedana as soon as possible, convert her to Muslim and secure *Jannat* (heaven) for both of you."

"Oh come on pal, you're talking hogwash. Do you know what love is? It is above all castes and creeds and beyond human egomania and narrow-mindedness and all your jingoist thoughts what you call as jihad come nowhere close to love," Naved explained.

"But there is no likelihood of love between a Muslim and a Hindu; a Hindu won't let you be his son-in-law straightforwardly and willingly. It's a facet of Islamic jihad so that Islam augments by leaps and bounds. You just take for instance, Naved bhai that your father goes to Vedana's dad with the proposal of marriage of you two, what do you think Vedana's father will do when he hears this? Will he just ask him to print the cards of your marriage? No! He will say 'NO' politely, and yes, politely because he works at your dad's clinic under him. He will then straight-away go and fix a meeting with the Bajrangdal men in the temple and Vedana will be walled in until her life-long union with somebody else, followed by your turn to get battered."

"Oh! Come on, my friend, nothing such is gonna happen; moreover your trash-talk just bears my mind off. Vedana loves me more than herself and she won't let come to pass anything like that. And the way you think about Hindus is wrong, they're humans too and in India we live among them."

"It's your misunderstanding, Naved............

....This country's ours and we've made it, it's us not them who are behind the identity of the nation. The pride of the country; the Taj Mahal, the Qutab Minarate, the Lal Quila (Red Fort), the Buland Darwaja and so on are all the works of our Muslim kings. All this is what makes this country worth its praise; they will have to tolerate us as we have made and decorated their home."

Fed up with Taufique's groundless refrainic argot and pusillanimity, Naved thought of telling him some real things about the country.

"They are all weak reasons and the Muslim kings, you're talking about came from central Asia and East Asia empty handed. They dug out of all the riches of the country and went back to their folds and a few of them who didn't go back like Baber and some others, ruled and fleeced our country. Take Baber for instance, he came to India from Iran with a company of men-at-arms and horses. What he found was a place which, no doubt, was well off but was divided into fragments, all of whom were at brawl with one another in the name of castes, classes and supremacy. He returned to Iran immediately to come back again with a fully-fledged army of assailants. They attacked from place to place and massacred millions of Hindus. Another thing I'd like to tell you that Islam is hardly a fourteen hundred years old faith which originated from Arab and the nearby African countries, from where Muslim assailants came to India (Pakistan and surrounding countries) and forced Islam upon our forefathers who were undoubtedly Idolatrous. All the works that you're talking about like the Taj Mahal or the Qutub Minarate were all places of worship of the Hindus, the Buddhists and the Jains. Have you ever seen the Qutub Minarate minutely? Just go there and witness how the carved out images of Lord Ganesha and other Hindu deities on the walls, the gables and the pillars have been hammered down and distorted. Most of our Mosques have been erected on the ruins of the temples.

Islam is, no doubt, an excellent faith of the world and the reason, it outgrew fast was that it excluded casteism or racism, foolish mumbo jumbos and the confusing paganism.

Hidnu dharma alias Sanatan dharma is in the worst situation, amazingly enough more than half of its followers are unaware of the fact that their faith is called Sanatan, their plight is so that despite following one faith they have apportioned themselves into countless races and communities grossly. And much to your happiness, they don't step down from slaying their own people from different castes; they are killing one another on the grounds of castes and *gotras* in one place, and languages and regions in another. Now see, what is happening in Maharashtra; Marathis are Hindus and I think most of the Biharis are Hindus too, but you know how they all are maltreated and shoved out by the Marathis. Where would such discarded people go now? These are the people in history who with no way out came to Islamic faith as Islam has always been a soothing hub for the downtrodden and outcast people.

Remember the recent happening at Kanpur? A Hindu dalit woman, Maya Devi was knocked up and was not allowed to enter a hospital of the *Swarnas* (upper class) community and as a result she died outside the hospital after delivering baby and after a few minutes the baby too left the 'High World'.

These are only small insights about the Hindu mind and community. But things are different for us, and for the Hindus who became Muslims. They had all undergone such maltreatment, dejection and airs, and Islam relieved them.

In Islam, Allah is the supreme power, and without His command not a single leaf moves but suffering is no less here as well. This faith, the foundation of which was laid upon unity, equality, peace and justice, today is tumbling down the social system because of its followers. The Muslims, who consider themselves to be followers of prophet

Mohammad, He Who symbolise equality in all walks of life, are stuck in the bog of communism. Islam's divided into two communities: the *Shias* and the *Sunnis* and further there are incalculable sects; that are seen to be high and menial.

The numerous so-called elite Muslims have compelled their own community people to become down and debased by tagging them as low caste. This has been smashing the ideal identity and objective of Islam. I love my country together with my faith because of all its good points but it doesn't mean I hate others.

Anyway yaar, I got carried away by emotions, and that is why I've spoken so much. To my mind Indian Muslims love their nation more than Hindus do and this is only because of our patriotic and religious instinct. Muslims are happy only in the UK, the USA and in India as they are under others there and here too, in all the Muslim countries barring the UAE and very few others, the condition of Muslims is pathetic in all regards. These dunder heads cannot make a good democracy; they can only be driven by dictatorship. Take example of Iraq, Egypt and Afghanistan, they were better off before they were freed from the dictators. Now imposing democracy on them by a Western country is ruining them to worse.

Maybe Islam's got some different meaning in your way of thinking but count on me, the real Islam teaches us the lesson of love, brotherhood, sacrifice, unity, humanity and kindness, besides jihad with which you interpret Islam doesn't mean intermarrying a Hindu girl or to injure someone, it simply implies spreading the message of love and brotherhood all over the world so that human who's become mundane man or rather beast, becomes more humane and justifies the meaning of being in the world making the world a more beautiful place for all creatures to live," he perorated fit to kill.

Taufique was listening to all the scintillating talkathon, Naved hobnobbed, so perspicaciously as if a child was sitting in class frightened and the class being attended by the principal. Though their behavior and characters were poles apart, they were good friends and Taufique respected Naved very much for his indubitable approach to life. He knew when Naved didn't speak, he didn't speak but when he began, he didn't hold back anything, and said a lot of incandescent things which are irresistible, so he was sat uttering sotto voce and listening to Naved. Taufique by nature was not a person who could mutely allow anyone to speak even for one tenth of an hour. Anyway both of the friends had talked enough and Naved hurried home. Both said Goodbye to each other and took their way home.

The incident fuelled the love between Naved and Vedana.

6

Impromptu Admission

One day Naved went to Vedana's college to pick her up where several young Hindu fuddy-duddies hindered his way and lambasted him animally because now he was at the radar of the Hindu boys in her class. While laming him up, they were yelling,

"Finish off this obnoxious bastard; he has spoilt one of our girls."

Naved was not of pugnacious nature, he got wounded but this episode stirred him deep inside. It was really an untoward experience for him. He was again unable to figure out whether it was a transgression for a Muslim to fall in love in Hindusthan. He had already been beaten twice before her and now he was feeling pretty dishonoured, disgraced and lonely. She on the other side was unable to move a straw, be that as it may, her will to withstand as two of the boys were from the same street that she lived in. All that she could do was watch desperately. He had to run away from the scene to save his life. He did not want to go home because his father had already presaged him that there could be no love between temple-goers and mosque-frequenters, so he cudgeled his brains and concluded to go to Taufique's. Three top buttons of his shirt were broken and there was a lump below his right eye. The fight had left him all black and blue. He could not escape by calling it a mere accident at home, so he reached his babyhood crony's domicile.

He fortunately found Taufique home, who was about to leave for the market. He blew his top when he saw his chum in such a dreadful state; he was thrilled by his pitiful condition. He held back his programme and asked Naved what had happened with him. Naved leveling himself gave him the whole account and that made Taufique fly off the handle and he bawled rambunctiously,

"Hmph!!! Those bloody damn kafirs, just tell me who they are. I won't let them go scot free, I will put them all in anvil............. Bah, oedipals!"

"Hold it bro, they are many and they own the country, we can do them no harm. Please don't just fly into rage. First and foremost get my shirt stitched and then bring me some medication for bump below my eye."

Naved was smarting from great contrition, he was nearly freaked out, yet Taufique was trying to nab his feelings and to solve it.

"You've trapped a 'Saffron' girl and you really need to be watchful and on your guard against such foxy rascals. These Hindu boys are muck and since you are Allah's child they are going to abhor you. They won't even see you with a Hindu girl let alone marrying one. One thing that you can do is that you don't bring yourself in by the name of Naved. Instead take any name like Bablu, Sonu, Monu, Raju, Goldy, Pintu, Bobby, Bunty and so on. And from today on I'll also start calling you Pintu; you start tying a red thread around your wrist and put on a tilak on the forehead that will make you appear like a tufty boy, then these Kafirs won't say you anything because they will think you are a one like them," put forward wily Taufique.

Naved took in what his pal had been speaking about for long. Earlier he could never make head or tail of what he said but now he decided to follow his buddy blindfoldedly. He began to fasten a *kalawa* (a religious red wristband) around his wrist by stealth, and when people at home inquired about it, he got off by saying that it was a friendship band gifted by a comrade.

Over time Naved gained by bearing a Hindu identity and he met Vedana without any fear or shilly-shallying. Years went by and during the period their love became so strong that severance between the two was no less than extinction.

But there was something else scriptural for them in their kismet. One night Pandit ji caught Vedana talking to Naved on the phone at an odd hour. No sooner had she seen her dad than she put the phone off; but she didn't know that he had been eavesdropping to their tête-à-tête for sometime long.

"It was a friend of mine," she rapped out nervously.

"I didn't ask you who it was," tears popped up in his eyes.

"I'm not sorry about whom you were talking to but about that you taught your father how to suck eggs," he continued.

"I'm penitent for that, dad!" she sprang out of the bed to enfold her father.

"Sorry...... I'm sorry," she burst out in tears sobbing and shivering, she told her father that she was talking to Naved.

"Naved......!!!?"

It came as a revelation to him and he had his feet knocked off.

This was the difficult moment of his life and he was awe struck as to how this all happened? And more importantly................ When? He looked at his daughter with non-expectation. Might his mind get broken down! On one hand was his teary-eyed daughter who was very dear to him but the society, his reputation and name was on the other. Desperation and ghastliness reflected clearly on his face.

Vedana realised the situation and began to bawl loudly. She wanted her father to say something and so she insisted that he spoke to her.

In the meantime *Panditain* woke up too and when she harked all the cry and clamour, she ran to see what was going on. When she reached there she could not figure out anything. She embraced her daughter in a hug and asked Pandit ji what they were doing.

Pandit ji stood like a statuette!!!

“Nothing! Everything is okay,” he exhaled after a while. But *Panditain* was not silly. Her eyes were filled with the lachrymal fluid and she screamed in a mess-making way.

“Just tell me what the matter is?”

“Take Vedana along to your room and she will tell you each and every detail, I don’t know anything,” replied he with asperities.

“OK, you go to your room first and she’s coming with me.”

And the mother daughter dyad moved to a room, and Pandit ji moved to his room. *Panditain* didn't wait even for the smallest unit of time and as they entered the room she said caressingly,

"Start honey!..................Don't pull your punches, my child."

Hearing this, Vedana burst into tears.

"I was talking to Naved on phone and dad espied this," she uttered.

These words were enough to drain off all color from the face of *Panditain*, yet she asked with affection.

"Was there something seminal at this sluggish hour in the night?"

"You just stop shedding tears first," said *Panditain* cuddling Vedana.

This time Vedana couldn't help herself and let out what she had held for long. In the heat of the moment she could not flinch from telling her mother what she was not supposed to disclose. She got things off her mind by stating her mother in a flurry of excitement that she loved Naved, and with tear drops in her eyes; she got her mother to swear that she would not unfold anything to her dad. *Panditain* was heart struck and felt as if some mountain had fallen over her. It was an acid test for her.

Her ears became unreceptive to this bolt from the blue, yet she restricted herself and asked,

"When was it established?"

"When it happened, I can tell you mother but how???............. I may not answer; it's been around five years now."

"Now, just put an end to it and get Naved off your mind," avowed the mother after a while in tranquility.

The easier it was for her to hear the harder it was to follow.

"Mother, your daughter is never going to do something that will put you to shame," assuaged Vedana holding on to her mother blubbering and weeping.

"But please don't tell father anything."

"Done, but now I shouldn't hear anything like this, nothing like this should recrudesce; and your mobile will be with me now," saying so *Panditain* moved to the kitchen to get some water.

She came back with a glassful of water for Vedana and then asked her to go to bed. *Panditain* fell asleep soon but sleep was miles away from Vedana's ocular-room, she went on with sobbing throughout the night. Her eyes were beset with Naved rather than sleep; even the thought of a life without him scared her. So she suffered unknown jimjams all night long.

'Where would Naved be if not in her life...............................!?'

Thoughts like this were giving her heart jerks.

"Oh no, I can't live without him," she murmured and got up. And as she got up she saw the face of her mother lying along and what was her promise to her, reflected in her memory, and she lied down again.

Moments appeared like years for her. She wanted to clasp her mother and weep.

But no! She got down from the bed and went up to the roof. She was at her wits' end.

"O God, please help me. The time is really hard and distressing for me. Please give your child strength and forbearance, I am in a fix and kindly extricate me from this impasse."

She prayed staring at the open blue; she was restless and was rambling to and fro on the roof incessantly. She was not able to focus her mind on anything so she returned to her room. She took a hard-board mounted picture of Lord Ram off the wall and clung to it on her heart.

"O Lord, give me strength," she prayed.

She pulled a chair close to her bed inconspicuously, put the picture of Lord Ram on it to have it in sight. She didn't want to see it from a distance so she again picked it up and adhered it to her heart. She sensed as if God was consoling her, it made her feel a little disburdened and in this bedlam she couldn't realise when she had nodded off.

In the morning she got up with the first ray of the sun. Without Naved the world looked vain and empty. He was associated with each and every thing and moment of her life. Anyway she strived to control herself and concentrate on study as her BEd examinations were fast approaching. Finally she busied herself preparing for the upcoming examination.

7

Two Doctors

On the other canvas Rajeev's BDS and Sabiha's MBBS also got completed and the same happened to their intimacy which had turned into affection with time. When they'd sunk deep conversing with each other into the deep of love, was a mystery. They had made promises not to separate ever. They went back to their respective homes.

In their families, nobody was aware of their relationship.

Having cracked a competitive exam, Sabiha got job in a Government Medical College, and Rajeev began to sit with his father at his clinic. Now they were well settled and so were planning about their marriage. Sabiha became a lecturer of gynaecology in Muzzafarnagar Medical College. She kept in touch with Rajeev. He also loved to speak to her whenever he got time.

They doted on each other; but somewhere in their hearts a qualm was ceaselessly vexing them that their relationship was between the two opposite poles of the society; one is South Pole and another the North Pole, they knew not only their biological parents but social parents also would stop them from being one but they didn't have any other way out but to tell their parents.

They deeply contemplated as to how to unseal, when and whom to unseal? They did not get any way out. They duo were very busy. In Rajeev's family, talks about his marriage were very common. Every time Rajeev put off his nuptial matters, saying that he had not come of the age of being matrimonially responsible. Sabiha too didn't deliberate at home because of Naved's matter as she knew it was going to add to misery in her family.

8

A Step into Future

Naved was lost in his studies and knew nothing about what had become of Vedana, he made an effort to contact her on her mobile but it was switched off. He was unaware of the throe she was going through. It was not easy for her to survive without him yet she had made up her mind boldly to keep him at arm's length. She didn't talk to him in this regard but she just began to fly blind of him, though she remembered him every moment.

After a couple of days she got her cell phone back. But she tried neither to answer his calls nor to meet him in deference to her parents' wish.

Naved, at first thought things would be normal but after some days he realised a change in Vedana. She, who'd never missed a single call of him, was now not answering any of his calls. When Naved found it difficult to hold on any longer, he intended to look into the reason.

He called her up from a public call office and unbeating about the bush asked the reason of being so indifferent.

"Nothing, there is nothing that you are thinking about. I am so busy at home and sometimes the mobile is in silent mode so I just couldn't attend it."

"Don't take me for a ride."

"I'm not befooling you."

Vedana tried to leave it out of account but Naved'd observed a big veer, and there was no way out for him but to believe her. With a light breath he accepted what she said but somewhere in his heart there was misgiving, and he gave a promise to himself to get the bottom of it.

With the passage of time Vedana gave up meeting him. But it was pretty hard for her as the more she struggled to walk away from him corporeally the more she came closer to him emotionally. Now she was obsessed with him all the time. She did her best to refrain herself and didn't meet him for two months. But there is a limit to everything. One day Naved asked her whether he should marry someone else as being pressured by his parents; and the moment she heard this, she broke down. She got beside herself with the excitement and told him all what had happened. He was sad to know how she had cloaked things from him.

"This means you do not trust me and I'm no one to you," rages Naved.

"I trust you the most and I'll see you tomorrow, but please don't speak anything like that. I can't live without you."

"We'll meet at the Sharma's Juice Shop."

"No"

"Somewhere else where we can talk easily and comfortably, I've to tell you so many important things," she continued.

"In privacy?"

"Yeah"

"I don't know a private place, Vedana.........let me think............................

I have.......er................if you don't mind."

"Where?"

"Chez my friend, Taufique"

"Taufique???........"

"Do you mind?"

"No...... Why should I, if you are with me?"

"OK! I will just talk to my pal and let you know soon and untill then take care! And remember.... be it any trouble or impediment, I am not going to slight you, I'm with you till my last breath," declared he.

"I love you, Naved! Love you a lot! Please don't ever lead me up the garden path," urged she.

"I won't! I'm with you, forever. I'll make the bandobast for tomorrow".

"Achcha, inform me soon".

"Achcha! Achcha! Love you! Bye!"

Naved was a shy person, he didn't have many friends so he called up Taufique. After a brief small talk he came to the bottom line huskily.

"I've to meet Vedana tomorrow. Can you help me to find somewhere to meet her, friend?"

It was as if an unasked wish had been answered for fiendish Taufique.

"She's Hindu, get her here and have your own way and don't let her go until you sanctify her".

Naved lent no ears to Taufique's out of the ordinary words.

"Do you really have a tryst or not, tell me simply?" Naved asked once more.

"Trysts are in plenty for this sacred act. I've been trying to explain you. Come whenever you want to, there's a garret down here unused. You can come tomorrow anytime," said busybody.

"Achcha, *Khuda Hafiz,*" closed Naved.

"*Khuda Hafiz,*" Taufique.

Naved was about to ring up Vedana but she called him before that.

"You've just got an amazing timing!" said Naved surprisingly.

"Have you arranged something for tomorrow?" Vedana meddled.

"I've just had a discussion with Taufique and if you don't mind, we can meet there," said Naved.

"I don't have any problem at brother Taufique's. He has perpetually been helpful..........fine....... I've to prepare meals; I put down the phone now lest somebody should see me. I see you tomorrow at 3 o'clock sharp, I'll be there at *Sharma's* and you pick me up from there," she cleared.

"Done! I'll be there. Take care, au revoir".

"Say something to give life to me," requested Naved.

"Tomorrow, please, please ...."

THE NEXT DAY:

"Oh come on dear! I've been waiting for you for over an hour. Where were you?" asked Vedana.

"Where else? I'm here on dot. May be you have arrived earlier........... Sharma ji, get us two lemonades please," Naved placed an order. Both took lemonade and then homed in on Taufique's place. He was at home waiting for them. As they reached there, he ushered them to the garret.

"Tea, coffee or anything, you want, just call me. And *bhabhi,* you too," said evil-designed Taufique closing the door.

He left them both in the room and went himself upstairs.

"So...What happened at home? What are they saying?" Naved broke the silence.

Vedana didn't utter anything rather she just caressed Naved and began to cry passionately. That's the first time both of them felt so close to each other.

"I'll stand by your side until I breathe last," he repeated fondly, "but promise me that you won't desert me too".

She embraced him tight in response, "I can't live sans you."

And as time passed they duo fell into each other ignorant of everything else and by the time they became conscious they had stepped into an all new world of love and now separation was no less than cremation for them.

"Please don't leave me," now she wood.

"Never, ever," he voiced.

That day instead of talking about future, they entered into it; and when evening came about they couldn't know. Vedana should have been at home by then but she desired to stay back with Naved.

"Don't be woebegone. If you stand by me, I'll take care of the rest," he put in affectionate words.

After some time Naved dropped Vedana home. She was not so happy that day and as she stepped in, she came across her father. Her heart beat hard when she saw her dad before her as she had broken the biggest ethical promise she'd made to her parents. Her father's sight stirred her from deep inside. She didn't look into his eyes and straight moved to her room. She was not able to look into anyone's eyes at home; she'd become so isolated at her own house. She felt guilty inside as she was no more her father's daughter. She had become somebody to someone else. She didn't come out of her room, and with an excuse of being under the weather, fell into sleep early and didn't take dinner either. She maintained the same mood for several days. She wanted to steal eyes from everyone. At home she pretended as if she was thinking no more of Naved and going to discard him soon but the truth now was more blood-curdling as now she met him once a week and they straight away went to the love nest at Taufique's house to enjoy togetherness. And this way she deceived herself too with her parents. She loved him more than anything so she didn't stop meeting him. But such things can't hide for long from the eyes of the society. One day she was seen with Naved by someone.

9

Hadji ji's Interdict

On the other hand, some Dr R.K. Verma came to Rajeev's father with the marriage proposal for his daughter Rashmi Verma. Rajeev's father didn't deny as he had a good rapport with Dr R.K. Verma. He spoke to Rajeev about it and made it clear that he wanted him to marry Rashmi. Rajeev being on crossroads, got stuck between a 'yes' and a 'no'.

His father directed him to go to Dr R.K. Verma's home to see Rashmi but Rajeev put it off by saying that he had some important work and so he wouldn't go. He requested his parents to visit Dr Verma without him with a promise that he would go soon to see the girl.

Dr Chander Kumar found the girl so suitable that he finalised the marriage without Rajeev's consent. A duel happened in his mind but he did not utter a word. Back home, he showed her photo to Rajeev and declared,

"We have finalised the girl."

Rajeev got upset but he did not reveal it.

He called up Sabiha and told her about the episode.

"Are you going to leave me?" she uttered tensefully.

Rajeev turned speechless. Having puzzled about it for a while, he suggested that she should discuss the matter at home and assured her not to be worried about him.

"In case they agree, it's fine, if not, we'll knock the court."

Sabiha didn't have mettle to talk to anyone at her home nevertheless she gathered courage and decided to speak to her brother not directly but in a crafty way. Though Dr Amanullah and Naved were open-hearted, yet she knew that it was not a trouble-free issue, it was the matter of societal importance.

She began to talk to Naved about Vedana. She asked how Vedana was and how all was going on. He was flabbergasted to know that Sabiha knew so much about Vedana as he invariably tried to keep the issue from his sister. When he intended to learn, she acted smart by saying.

"This is the only job of a sister to know more and more about her handsome bhai."

Since she was not so interested in his matter, instead of wasting so much of time on rubbish, she directly reached the point.

She asked, "*Bhaijaan*, does religion really play a paramount role in love?"

He thought she must be asking this in his context, so he replied abruptly in a philosophical style.

"Love is itself a religion which is the gist of all the religions, and people who keep religion away from love or vice versa, do not know the real meaning of being religious............."

"So you are going to wed Vedana?" she asked him stopping him in between and having collected prowess got to this also if she could marry a Hindu boy too.

Naved, unaware of her contrivance, said,

"If the boy hails from a good family and loves you then what else is needed, however religion is all about goodness of a person, and if a person is immaculate by heart and brain means he is religious and then recognising the name of the religion becomes irrelevant and immaterial."

Hearing so, Sabiha did not say anything else and bidding goodnight she retired to her room.

Naved reflected for a while and suddenly reached her room, he wanted to know why she was talking like that because she usually remained reticent and enjoyed her own involvements. She was not so much mixed up in the family. She had been in hostel up to twelfth class. And now just after completion of her study, she got a job in a government medical college.

She was taciturn by nature and a to-the-point girl.

He had never heard her before talking like that so he thought it better to go to her and ask.

"Sabiha, why did you ask this?"

She, having understood his tone, concealed her expressions and uttered,

"Can I talk to Vedana?"

Naved unexpectedly asked in astonishment,

"Why?"

"Just like that!"

Naved was shocked to know that his sis knew so much about Vedana as until then Naved had always tried to keep it from his family. He once again asked how she knew so much about him.

"Leave it brother I even know that you call her 'Blob of Butter'..........Tell me when you are taking me to her."

"Hmmm............. Meeting, I'll think about it later, but if you really wish, you can talk to her right now."

He called up Vedana and requested her to speak to his sister Sabiha. Vedana already knew a lot about Sabiha. Naved handed the phone to Sabiha and she headed to another room talking on the phone. While talking she alluded her affair with Rajeev in a few words. Vedana didn't take long to recognise that Sabiha was in love with Rajeev. As she was in love too, she well understood her feelings. Sabiha asked Vedana to explore Naved's heart about her sister's inter-religion match. She assured her that she would ask everything tactfully and would not let anything happen which is not in favour. She assured Sabiha to consider herself as her elder sister and not to lose sleep. She asked Sabiha to hand over the phone to Naved.

"Your sister is very sweet and cute."

"After all she is the sis of the smartest guy in the world."

"Ha ha ha.........what a joke! ....I'm to cook food and help mum with the washing up. Bye! Night! I'll call you tomorrow now."

The following day Naved was curious to know what'd happened the previous day between Vedana and his sister on the phone. He himself phoned at around 11 o'clock. As soon as she picked the phone, he posed,

"What did you cook yesterday?"

"No, it was nothing so vital; she simply asked when and how we'd marry?.......................Well, Naved, tell me one thing as you are Muslim and I'm Hindu and we're going to get immingled. Is it doable for Sabiha too to get married with a Hindu boy? Can I get a match for her in my clan? She is a very statuesque girl," Vedana verbalised accordingly.

Naved was above all these constrictions.

He said, "Marriages are family matters and provided I'm all in all, it won't be an issue for me. Butttttt .... for marriage, only father can see a boy though he'll finalise the boy after consulting all family members, especially Sabiha. After all it is a question of a life long knot so for this papa's consent is inevitable."

Vedana listened to all this in quiescence.

"Hmmm" ..... She broke her silence and said,

"Speak to your father and explore whether he agrees to such a match or not."

"O! Aye, it's a good idea, I'll try to know indirectly but before that let me know about our future?" he spoke drolly.

At this she disconnected the phone saying, "I love you."

Naved had a word with his father about Sabiha's marriage but he couldn't dare to ask if it could be done with a Hindu boy. His father made it clear marriage is the matter of family's honour. It's not one man's job; it takes place with the consent of all.

Naved resumed saying, "Papa, I know an apt boy for her but he is Hindu."

"Hinduuuuu!!!" Doctor Sahib paused for a while and then broke in,

"I fear if your uncle allows this interblast match, however I'll talk to him."

In the evening Doctor Sahib went to his elder brother and in discourse had a trace of Naved's proposal.

"Okay!" came an all surprising reply by Sadiqullah who was in the habit of vomiting venom against Hindus by and large.

"It can happen," suddenly his tone revolutionised and he spoke standing and hanging his achkan on a nail.

"Bhai Amanullah, this can happen," picked up worshipful Hadji ji enigmatically where he left off, "but only if the boy is ready to adopt Islam; otherwise we have the right on our daughter's present, past and future as we have borne her, we can make things happen in our favour."

It was a very diplomatic reply.

Naved told Vedana about this.

Now it was unambiguous for Sabiha that her espousal with Rajeev was not a child's rattle. Thereover Rajeev's marriage proposals were coming in full swing. And Rajeev couldn't dare ask his father. However Sabiha was unremittingly asking him to take an idea from his father about what to do?

Eventually Rajeev gathered steel to speak out his heart to his father. His father gainsaid bluntly adding if by chance it happened, he would not comply with it because they were Hindu.

"My son, do one thing, just call a halt to this unreligious alliance and forget her ad infinitum."

It was not easy for Rajeev, therefore he, instead of toeing the instructional line, planned to marry Sabiha in court.

10

Visits of Mr Goyal

One day my elder brother Professor V K Goyal went to Panditji's house. He is a retired Professor of Zoology in the SN College, a liver of the same *mohalla* and an active associate of the Rashtriya Svayam Sevak Sangh.

"Namaskar Pandit ji, the girl's grown up now. Don't you ever think of her wedlock, bro?" he asked Pandit ji.

"Namaskar Goyal Sahib, she's your daughter too bhaisaab! Just tell us some good match. We're not going to take long. Who likes a grown-up daughter at home?" uttered Pandit ji.

"Brother, what children want has become decisive today. So just ask your daughter whether she likes someone and inform me by the evening on phone what she says. I'll tell you several good proposals," said Goyal Sahib.

"What do you say Goyal Sahib? Your daughter is not of that kind. What I finalise for her she will accept. She is not very open in these matters; she doesn't like to talk about her nuptial issues. Whenever I discuss the matter with her mother, she blushes away."

"Well, that's good, now I will send you some proposals. OK then.... I beg to leave now," said Goyal Sahib to Pandit ji, "till we meet again. Namaskar."

Pandit ji spoke to *Panditain*, "Now it's time that we see off Vedana in marriage. Goyal Sahib will send us some proposals. I don't have much understanding; it's your job to size them up."

"Yeah, let them come, and about the boy she will choose one. Today boys and girls cotton to each other first, other things are left for afterwards."

In the evening when Vedana returned home, Pandit ji put it forth,

"Listen daughter, it's time that you enter into new phase of life. Prof Goyal of the RSS came here today and he's got some matches for you."

Vedana for a moment lost her mind but soon she modified herself and remarked,

"Dad, what you do will be inevitable for me. You can send your daughter wherever you want to and she'll say nothing."

Daughter's words get Pandlt ji in high-spirits,

"I'm not going to send my dear daughter just anywhere, I'll do my best and the rest is the will of God. Only He knows what He wishes ...."

"Why don't you cook kheer today; it's been a long time that we haven't eaten anything sweetish and do add some dry fruits to it. Just do it if you can!" elated Pandit ji turned to *Panditain*.

"O sure, I will," said she.

"And just tell me right away if you want me to get something because I won't be going outside later when the Indo-Pak cricket match starts," said Pandit ji switching on the TV.

"No nothing! I have got the whole shebang in kitchen," replied *Panditain* going into the cooking cell.

The match started and Pandit ji got busy watching it, *Panditain* got busy in the kitchen and Vedana on phone surreptitiously. She's now firm at heart not to live without Naved. They had come too far, too deep. Pandit ji there was watching match and doing commentary too. Although he was not biased, yet India's winning on the pitch of war was no doubt looked forward to.

Anyway, things were going on as usual – Panditji's job, Vedana's study and *Panditain's* puja-*path*.

Some days later Professor Goyal came up with a proposal. The boy worked for an MNC and belonged to Modinagar; he was financially sound and lived alone in Noida.

Pandit ji described him before his daughter.

"There's a boy Sandeep. Mother and father both are government teachers. If you say we'll invite them this Sunday, the day when the clinic is closed would be better. Is it fine? Take care, and tell me, I'll do it by Sunday," Pandit ji informed *Panditain* with a slight chortle.

"Oh come on! When you are at home your cricket matches never end. What'll you do then?"

"I'll manage; I'm not a batty cricket-aficionado."

Well, Pandit ji talked to Professor Goyal and fixed on Sunday to call Sandeep and family.

When Vedana told Naved about this, he turned pale with evil forebodings. She relieved him by saying that she would look after it and that he shouldn't be anxious. But it was Naved who's not able to figure what's happening.

"Please don't bemuse me. Do you want to leave me and breach all promises?" sighed Naved.

"Nay! What do you say? I'm not breaking any promises; you just see for yourself. When they make tracks, I'll give you a call....," Vedana infused courage.

"Achcha," Naved only replied.

"Welcome, Professor Sahib, I'd just been waiting for you," said Pandit ji at their arrival.

"Oh come on Pandit ji! How's possible that you call us and we don't turn up".

"Well, please have a seat."

They all took a pew in parlour.

"I'll introduce you to all. This is Pt Bholaram and this is his wife: Vedana's parents and this is Master ji Mr Omprakash and this is Satyawati, his wife. You both are teachers in a govt school. This yonker is Sandeep Kaushik, their worthy son, working for an MNC, working good and the only son; and they are blessed with everything."

"Arey *bhabhiji*, where're you going? Ask your daughter and she'll get what it is. You just sit here and talk to each other. My job was to bring you all together, the rest is up to you as you both are much the same to me," said Professor Sahib.

"Professor Sahib, what do you say? It's great that people like you are there in the society!" Pandit ji barged in.

Professor Sahib thus facilitated a good conversation between the two parties. He inquired everything from both of the sides for both of the sides. Meanwhile *Panditain* got up and moved to call Vedana to come over. Vedana who had big eyes appeared with her eyes down as if a half risen moon in less astral sky peering through the clouds. Any mature boy couldn't say no for marrying her after beholding her once. At the first sight, one could see all that added to the womanly charm and the same thing happened to Sandeep too; he was left spell-bound at the very first view of Vedana but her heart was somewhere else. She paid abnormal inattention to Sandeep and failed to bring herself to do or to say something.

"Vedana, if you two want, you can sit alone and talk to each other," said Professor Sahib. But she didn't take any interest and within minutes she stood up and walked inside.

"May be she has reddened, *bhabhi* will go and ask her whether she cottons to Sandeep," Professor Sahib poured words.

Panditain strolled inside to know her mind.

She pronounced, "No."

Shocked and chocked *Panditain* asked the reason.

She added, "He is no white like a crow."

Panditain dropped from the ninth cloud; the whole inside turned pensive, she wondered what to say to them now?

She contemplated for a split second and joined them,

"Right now she's not able to say anything. Why don't we carry on later?"

"This would be better to see how the land lies," Professor Sahib broke in, "You two parties discuss the things at home in detail."

"I'll discuss with my brother," said *Panditain*.

"That's fine."

"Okey doke Pandit ji, good to meet you! We'd like to leave now".

"You great sir, it was good of you to visit us!" said Pandit Bholaram with folded hands.

"See you soon, *Namastey* Pandit ji," said Professor Sahib departing.

"Wow! I liked the boy, the family is fine, all are well educated," Pandit ji chirped in pleasure, unaware of the fact that Vedana had already rejected the proposal.

Meanwhile Vedana turned out, "Dad, you see he's dark. Are you going to settle a boy like that for me? I don't like him at all."

Vedana's assertion cooked his goose and struck him dumb; he took it for something else. Yet he offset his mind and gave surety to her that without her 'yes' things wouldn't be advanced further.

"Oh! Come on sweetie! I won't just push you out like that anywhere. First I would want you to set your heart on the boy. I'll talk to Professor Sahib and work it out. Well see what we can do? After all you have to spend your life with the boy, so he should be your choice."

11

An Imbroglio

Came the day when Rajeev had to go to see Rashmi. His family members pressurised him to go and see her. In the wake of which, he went to see her. He informed Sabiha that he was going to see Rashmi in pressure and formality and after coming back he'd see a lawyer to know what and how to proceed further. He left to see Rashmi with his mother though they had already finalised her and were waiting for his approval.

Rashmi, an MBBS (Gynae) was a charming chic in her mid twenties; she was a svelte girl with blonde hair, petally lips, a sharp nose, a sweet smile and eyes as if naturally painted with kajal, she even outweighed Sabiha in looks. All these features added to her beauty. She was a perfect blend of corporal as well as cerebral beauty.

They reached there; welcomed warmly by Rashmi's family and had deliberations over future prospects.

Meanwhile Rashmi was called. She came and parked herself opposite Rajeev; he was unmoved by her beautiful aspects and rather overlooked her. Once or twice he raised his eyes, but always it was Sabiha's image which blocked his view. All of them sat talking to one another and sipping over tea.

"We've talked a lot; now let them have a discourse. Let's send them upstairs to terrace in order to know each other well. After all we are all here to get them united for keeps," suggested Rashmi's mother.

All acquiesced laughing. Rashmi's brother escorted them upstairs. Rajeev didn't have any interest in her. Now when he got clear and complete view of her, he was impressed at the very first sight, which's why he failed to prevent himself from saying.

"You seem to be superb in all aspects, it is a separate thing whether we are knotted or not but I would wish your future be bright like your face!"

Perhaps she was accustomed to hearing all this and so replied smilingly,

"Charming face can not beautify your destiny, but a good destiny is definitely a guarantee of a charming face."

Rajeev felt weird and wonderful having listened to this. He discerned a note of agony in her utterance. It seemed to him as if some pressure had affected her mind balefully. Though he was not interested in her, yet in courtesy he decided to ask what'd happened, what'd moved her so deeply and grossly.

"You are so beauteous and worthy that I don't think even God would have ever thought to put you in any adversity," Rajeev.

Rashmi, "You are right, Rajeev, it is not God; it's people who have classified me."

Saying so she jutted her right hand out and spoke,

"Rajeev, I know why you don't take interest in me and why you too will go rejecting me like others did."

Her eyes brimmed with tears and she moved to go downstairs.

Rajeev nudged her to stop,

"Why do you think so?" he asked.

"Oh! Leave it, please."

But the twinge in her voice pushed him to inquire into.

On this, Rashmi let things out, "Due to this amputated finger, everybody rejects me."

She resumed, "My uncle (mediator) kept it from you and your family but I won't like a conjunction to be made on the foundation of lie."

In passing, Rajeev received a message from Sabiha in his cell phone. It read:

"Uncle has appropriated my phone, I'm at his home. He is fixing my marriage somewhere else. Wait for me and take care."

Actually Sabiha's cousin had seen some electronic epistles to Rajeev in her cellular phone and it led her into the furnace of fury of her family members, specially her uncle Sadiqullah.

Rajeev could not make out what to do and what not, he was in a dilemma; he was on crossroads? He's going through an exam of life. He, in the twinkling of an eye called up Sabiha but her cell was switched off. He very hardly held himself up. But he didn't let Rashmi notice his distress. The time was tough for him. Hopesick Rashmi was standing quiet before him. He didn't think of anything; but suddenly got a brainchild.

He found his pain to be less significant in comparison to that of Rashmi. It has always happened to love; love has always undergone lots of trouble. But what was happening with Rashmi was neither good nor civil. Her misery was more intense than his. Holding himself he asked Rashmi.

"Why so?"

She revealed, "It is believed in Hindus that if body is incomplete, food offered to ancestors is not accepted by them, puja or any other oblation offered to God does not prove to be fruitful, so nobody has ever liked me; and all went refusing. And today perhaps you too................! And yes in case, you have mercy on me, your parents, as soon as they come to know, will cancel this proposal."

Rajeev was taken aback at Rashmi's heart distressing reality.

..............*PAUSE* ....

He phoned Sabiha once again but it was still switched off. He cooled his storming mind down and reflected that one's pain can be reduced only by standing in another person's pain which is more intense. He did what his heart said and he held her hand at once and declared,

"I'll not do so because your twenty per cent of normal finger does not matter to me."

"I'll stand by you."

These words brought smile on her face as though solaced by his demeanour.

It eased Rajeev's pain and he entered into a new realm. Both of them got downstairs and took the weight off their feet in the drawing room. Rajeev had a feeling of complacence on his face. All looked at him hopefully; and he viewed his mother with a positive outlook. He gesticulated towards his mother and she signaled Doctor Sahib to advance. Dr Chander stood and embraced R K Verma and said to him to approach a celebrant to fix dates for the next proceedings. He fixed on a date for the ritual of *maang bharai* on the spot. It was set on twelfth May and there were forty two days in between. The gathering ended at a very happy note. All bade *Namastey* to one another and dispersed.

Sabiha's condition was deteriorating day by day; she was not allowed to talk to anyone and confined to the length and breadth of the house. Her brain was being washed, it was made clear to her that 'marriage is a matter beyond, even speaking to kafirs is not less than a sin.'

Hadji ji was twenty four seven coaxing her to change her mind. For around twenty days she sojourned with her uncle at his house, she didn't have a cell phone so she couldn't reach Rajeev. Rajeev too tried few times to phone her but her cell was switched off. He was sure that Sabiha had been taken to Timbuktu, very far away from him. He'd known that Sabiha and his life together was not possible in this world so in the moment of pain he thought of lessening somebody else's pain as he found it a panacea for his broken heart.

Sabiha's mind was redesigned in such a way that when after around twenty days she went back to her hospital, she didn't desire to call up Rajeev. In fact now she didn't want to go to the trail of suffering. While going back home first day after hospital at six pm, she felt like crying as she was in the habit of calling up Rajeev at that time; it was her fixed time to talk to Rajeev. She tried once with trembling fingers but his phone was switched off. He had become an integral part of her life. Now sometimes she missed him a lot. Rajeev too didn't try to accost her but somewhere in the back of his mind it was there–

"How would Sabiha be? Where would she be?"

Nobody can overcome the mighty time and it was time that separated Sabiha from him and brought Rashmi closer. Rajeev was low at Sabiha's loss but he was satisfied for standing by somebody in pain. Eventually his marriage date was fixed. Both Rajeev and Sabina had given in to time and the latter was trying to be regular at her hospital. She got transferred from Muzzafarnagar to Khatauli Government Hospital that was on Delhi-Dehradun highway.

One day Rajeev planned to go to Muzzafarnagar, his in-laws. In fact he had to shop with Rashmi so he took his coupé and at four pm left for Muzzafarnagar. He'd informed to be back late at night to his parents. He left house and in fifteen minutes he reached highway, where his car began to talk to air and he to Rashmi (in imagination). His destination was Rashmi's house. He was about to reach the burg of Khatauli.

He saw a car parked suspiciously, half on and half down the road in the mud of the post-rain roadside, prima facie, it seemed to be a bit more than a fender bender. He slowed down and descried a boy lying on the roadside near to the car, imbued with blood. Being driven by the most refined characteristic of a human being, he applied brake to the car. He alighted the quadruwheeler and rushed towards the hurt man. As soon as he knelt down to feel his pulse, he received a sudden and powerful push on his back, and just the next moment he found himself in the grip of four squalid men. He could not make out what'd happened, he was completely taken into shock. What he saw was beyond belief; he saw that wounded man upping shaking down his clothes. Surprisingly enough he was quite well, he was not bleeding anywhere. Now Rajeev'd taken in all what he had entered into. He'd been conspired by the hooligans, he'd become the prey of road hold-up. Some more people come out from the sugar bush and began to hammer him. He wanted to withstand them but all in vain as they were more in number. He screamed blue murder but on the lonely road of charcoal and gravel his voice died unheard. They looted his watch, purse, mobile and fled in his car. Before leaving they'd beaten him till he lost his conscience, they ran away leaving him half dead.

He was hurt and bleeding. After they had gone, he tried to stand on twos but failed and fainted down again. Fortunately after around five minutes, a school bus passed from there that was going back to Khatauli, having celebrated an outing in Delhi. Some students caught his sight lying disserved and down at the roadside.

They shouted and had the bus stopped. In the bus were forty five students along with five teachers and vice principal. Two teachers got down the bus and went near him. Rajeev, getting the hoi polloi around him, first was afraid of them and slowly spoke,

"I don't have anything with me now."

The teachers comforted him saying that they were teachers and would take him to hospital. One of them went back to the bus and called the vice principal down. He telephoned the police and principal and at police's suggestion rushed him to the nearest government hospital in their bus. They directly rushed him to the civil hospital. One of the teachers Mr V P Singh explained all to the doctor-in-charge and got him admitted in the ICU inside of ten minutes. The police reached there and did their formality quickly so as not to hamper his treatment.

But, see the irony of fate and the wish of God! Rajeev reached the same hospital where Sabiha worked; though it was night and Sabiha did not take the graveyard shift. Rajeev had a severe head injury due to which he had lost his consciousness. His wound was stitched. He had lost enough of blood and now doctors needed blood for him. As goons had snatched everything from him so police were helpless and clueless about his identity. Police did not know him from Adam and did not have any other election but to wait for him to be resuscitated.

At 9' evening, he tried to turn over his body and opened his eyes ajar; he was feeling painful all over. Police saw a streak of hope and tried to collect information about him. He was not in the condition to speak a word. The police, thinking of getting his telephone number written, arranged a paper and he very hardly scrawled his landline number. Police dialed the number without procrastination.

His sister picked phone. On hearing about her brother's accident, she screamed perturbedly "Mum...........................mum.........mummmmmmmmm ....bhai.......... bhai is ...."

"What happened to Rajeev???"

Hearing about Rajeev, her mother lost her wits.

Meanwhile father also joined the bemoaning duo. He assuaged them and scuttled to Khatauli and at around half past eleven they all were in hospital. They discovered Rajeev sleeping unconsciously. Mr Verma conversed with the doctors present there; he was not fully satiated with his treatment. He talked to the police and got informed that his son had fallen victim to the road hold-up.

He aspired to take his son with him; but it being a police case, he was not allowed to leave hospital before making declaration. Rajeev's mother was bemoaning very badly. She too wanted to take him back to Meerut for better treatment. Police advised them to wait till he regained conscious to state what exactly happened to him. They had to assent to the police suggestion. They reluctantly stayed at the hospital. It was a restless night. All were anxious about Rajeev's condition. He was in medicinal effect but his parents kept on tossing the whole night.

From Muzzafarnagar, his in-laws had been calling him up since evening, but the phone was switched off. They were waiting for him. Eventually Dr R K Verma rang up his father. He held him up and decided not to tell this to Dr Verma.

He said, "Even I don't know where he is? Might have gone to some friend, you don't worry. As soon as I hear anything from his side, I'll inform you." They end the call at this.

But Dr Chander did not feel comfortable with not telling his kith the truth. He made up mind to tell him everything in the morning. They kept awake the whole night and with a hope came the morning. It had been a difficult night. It was the game of destiny that Rajeev was in the same hospital where Sabiha worked.

In the morning at 8, Sabiha came to hospital. She was not in the know about Rajeev's admission there; they didn't talk to each other in last one month. She turned up and directly advanced to her cabin. Rajeev was now out of the ICU and his parents had finished doing paper formality to take him back home. His father longed to take him to a private hospital before long.

Rajeev and Sabiha were again under one roof. Time had once again brought them close to each other. But time...................

Time lets only those things happen what it likes to. Time is the reef upon which all our frail ships of dreams are wrecked.

Being under one roof, they didn't even see each other. Once again they gave in to time. He had been relieved from the hospital. Time brought them closer but separated them unmet. He went back home and she on job.

After an hour of their departure, a photographer came to the hospital. Not finding anyone on the reception, he slunk into a cabin near reception. It was Sabiha's cabin.

He said to her, "Hello doc, I've brought pics of a patient ...."

"What's the name?"

"............ Ishshsh let me check.......it is Rajeev."

Sabiha received pics and placed them in a drawer.

"Patient Rajeev's pics".... "..............."

These words struck her mind. Intuitively, she opened the envelope in no time. What she saw was really unexpectedly shocking.

Time........... very powerful, it brought them closer and parted. Sabiha approximated the doctor to know more about Rajeev's incident. She brought his medical jurisprudential report from the doctor concerned to know more about his accident. She sat in her cabin and went through the report between the lines. Reading it all, her eyes got saturated with saline liquid. She felt a kind of tease in her heart. She noted his number from the file and called him up; but his mobile handset was off. After that she tried another number scribed on file which his father picked. On hearing father's voice, she disconnected it. She becked Kaka, an attendant, and told him make her talk to patient Rajeev. He dialed the number, brought Rajeev on line and handed phone to her. She heard his voice after a long month of thirty days. She didn't know what and how to say.

All that she adlibbed was,

"Rajeev"

Saying this she cut the phone and went AWOL from the hospital. Rajeev called her back in a jiffy but his call was picked by the attendant. Rajeev asked him about Sabiha.

Attendant said, "She's just left for home on some urgent job."

"Who're you? Why do you want her?"

Rajeev spoke tactfully, "My wife's health is serious and she's under Dr Sabiha's treatment; kindly give me her number."

Kaka gave Rajeev her number. He, before the expiry of a minute, called her up from his father's mobile. No sooner did she pick up than Rajeev began, "Sabiha, please don't disconnect; I'm badly wounded, my physical condition is really down. I was admitted to hospital for the whole night. I can't put stress on my brain, so kindly tell me-how and where are you? ...."

Being a medical lady, she knew it well how to treat a patient. Therefore she verbalised convivially,

"I'm all well and working in Khatauli hospital where you were last night. You please take care of yourself; I'll call you up after a few days. Well............... I'm not cross with you. You please be worry-free; I promise I'll call you up as and when I get time. Take care for the sake of all who love you. Bye.................."

Rajeev was not in the condition of speaking much so he kept himself to himself for next few days.

Rashmi and her family too came to know about that misadventure; they came running to Dr Chander' bhavan, took account of all that had happened and felt extremely sorry about that.

The time rolled by and now Rajeev was much better off and normal. Rashmi was in constant contact; she called him up almost every day, irrespective of it being sunny or rainy.

After he'd spoken to Sabiha, he felt it odd and atypical to talk to Rashmi.

Sabiha phoned after around five days and first asked after his health and then about his life, his marriage, and so on. When she got to know about his marriage that proposals were coming in myriad, she felt jolted deeply; but she didn't let it be grasped by Rajeev and continued.

"I'm your past; a person should advance forgetting his past. Those who are stuck to their past, can't progress in future."

Rajeev listened to everything circumspectly. He asked her about her life.

Sabiha pronounced, "No change, same life."

"Have you finalised a girl?" she asked interrupting him in the middle.

"There is nothing like that, only proposals are in swing and none has been finalised so far," he brushed aside craftily.

12

Ill-fated Decision

"Vimla, inviting a boy first and then saying 'no' like this, doesn't seem good; so the next time somebody tells us a match, we'll first ask for boy's photograph and show it to Vedana and will proceed only after," Pandit ji elucidated etiquettes to *Panditain*. She saw eye to eye as this was going to make her mind light and her work easier.

"Dad, ask for the horoscope too along with the snap. Once we see the snap and match the horoscope, we'll call them up," Vedana joined them.

"Humm bhai, Vedana is right, matching of horoscope is very important." "So from next time on we'll ask for the photograph and horoscope first and we'll arrange meeting only after papery satisfaction," *Panditain* added.

Pandit ji agreed to this with the proviso and was unaware of whatever was going on there in his daughter's cerebrocastle. And she this way bought time and made her job easier.

First she gave Naved the full account of the day and then assured him not to be troubled about the future. That day they didn't talk much; Vedana had to help her mom for the guests who were coming around. She thought how it was to loiter about things. This way she passed many proposals up. First she got the horoscope matched from her dad if that didn't match; she cancelled that proposal without even seeing the photograph if it did she found some faults in the boy's photograph, and so she was putting off the alliances. At times she pretended to be tense but actually thanked to her lucky stars; she let Naved know how she was cancelling all proposals. In this way, she rejected four matches in seven months.

When she didn't approve of even a single alliance suggested by Professor Goyal, he smelled a rat and concluded that that was indeed true, as he was apprised of earlier that the girl had an affair with Naved. She had already finalised her choice. But he couldn't unravel it in her house. He was associated with the RSS and there he met a girl by the name of Anu and shared how a Hindu girl had fallen prey to the black love-jihad; how she had been trapped and had advanced to become a Muslim. But he could do nothing because of lack of any solid evidence as the matter was so sensitive. So he thought it better to remain silent but he couldn't actually see an idolatrous sink into dirty and dreary bog of love-*jihad*. He disclosed there is love-*jihad* going on with thews and sinews all across India. Every year hundreds of Hindu girls are being spoilt and converted to Muslim faith. Muslim boys befriend them in false Hindu names and beguile them with their soft soap. And by the time the girls know the truth they are not the same what they used to be.

But this is what he cerebrates and how much reality it contains he only knows. He was not able to take any action because openly Vedana was ready for marriage but the only problem was that of a match of her choice. This continued for some days. He wanted to prevent Vedana from being a pawn in Naved's vicious *Jihadi* Plan. But how???

In the meantime Vedana and Naved advanced to marry as early as possible. Naved could take his dad into his favour but for Vedana it was a Herculean task; and this kept her so edgy and restless. She couldn't focus herself on anything; till now she had been managing by saying now and then that she followed her father. But Pandit ji had made it clear that he was going to finalise the very next proposal that would come up. This made her heart skip a beat. She hesitated to talk to her parents directly in this regard. She didn't find a way to do it; she thought of talking to her mom many times and looked for chances but as soon as she went to her, she broke down like a nanny goat before a tigress and all the stuff of her heart remained within. She talked about trifles and comes back.

One day a relative of Pandit ji expired and so he required some days' off. Dr Aman allowed him to leave. This was enough for Vedana to seek a chance out.

"So good of Doctor Sahib, who says Muslims are not good guys? Doctor Sahib has always supported us..........," Vedana blurted out to her mom, "Naved is also good," she moved on acquiring a little more daring.

Her mom rolled her eyes over as she heard the name of Naved.

"Mom, I don't mean that. Anyway, you tell me if it is possible that we get married?" Vedana breathed at once.

But *Panditain* took it easy, "See honey! If he were a Hindu or of any other caste, I'd go with you but he is a Muslim and wedlock between an outbred Hindu and inbred Muslim is never approved of; moreover these people don't do a good turn. The society will think us over the Muslims."

"But mom, it is us who make Hindus and Muslims. God doesn't discriminate between us when he creates us," articulated she, plussing a little more steel.

"You don't argue with me," her mom cut her short.

"If you have got something to say, talk to your father, don't bother me... .....Oh! God, the girl seems to have lost all her modesty," and *Panditain* walked away.

Vedana felt lonely and distressed; she didn't dare to talk to her dad so she typed a message and sent that to Naved.

"Naved ...."

Having received the message, he got traumatised. The message read,

"Good Bye."

He hurried to contact her but she didn't pick up the phone until he compelled her by swearing to do so.

He explained heavy-heartedly to her, "Please just talk to your dad because dads love their daughters; he'll unquestionably understand you. Please don't do such asinine things; counsel him and he'll catch on the right end."

"No, he won't, you please take care of yourself and marry somewhere else; my dad won't comprehend. If you want to go ....Please go. ...."

"Vedana, if I go, I won't go from your world but rather will leave the world," added Naved.

"Please don't say that; I can't go against my dad. He's always loved me and brought me up; he has never let my wishes remain unfulfilled."

"But ...."

"Please........ Why don't you get it into your head?" she moved on.

"Achcha! I do, Vedana, and just for your happiness if you want me to go away, I'll do that. Bye!" announced he and put the phone down and switched that off as well.

Oh God! For Vedana, it was really so painful, she endeavored to phone him back repeatedly but all she listened to was,

'The Idea number you are trying to call has been switched off. Please try later.'

And this message was just bumping her off. She prayed to God that Naved should turn his cell phone on. It seemed as if she was nearing her end; she ate nothing, she drank nothing. She was on tenterhooks and just trying to contact him.

When nothing occurred to her, she called Taufique.

"Please tell me something about Naved. It is 11:30 in the nocturnal time; his phone is switched off. He is cross with me, please get me to talk to him right away," begged she.

"You just don't worry. I'll call you back in ten minutes," said he and hurried to Naved's home as his phone was switched off.

Naved didn't live in the immediate vicinity. He hastened to his home. When reached there, Doctor Sahib opened the door.

"*Salaam Valekkum*, Uncle."

"*Valekkum Ahsalaam,* my son. Come in."

"Where is Naved, uncle?"

"Naved is at home; just come in."

"Naved................Naved.......," Doctor Sahib called.

When he didn't turn up; Taufique moved to his room followed by his father where he found him sleeping. When he ran his eyes around, he was surprised to see Naved had a wound in his hand that had been dressed.

He was a neighbour so he went there frequently.

"What happened to him?" Taufique asked Doctor Sahib.

"Bhai, he told me that he was slicing cucumber when he mishandled the knife. He has never sliced cucumber in his life before. What was the need for him to do it today that he sat down to slice cucumbers; Allah knows what happened? Why don't you ask him?"

Doctor Sahib, saying so, went back to his own room.

Taufique went near him to wake him up,

"What the heck are you doing here? You know Vedana's dying there calling you on and on; talk to her first and then tell me what the hell you have been up to? Hurry up, she was crying on the phone."

"O yea I will. I just got hurt," said Naved.

"Eww! You don't take me in, fuck that! Why don't you marry her in court? Let's see how his dad doesn't make you his son-in-law," flayed out incensed Taufique.

"Alright yaar, I'll just phone her. And you just go home, it's 12 o'clock midnight, you see."

"No, you're going to call her up right now, before me."

"See! I'm doing that."

"Yes! Why are you in torrent of tears?" she picked the phone up.

Seeing this, the go-between made a move.

"I just had an injury in my hand and so I took codeine and had been sleeping since."

"No! No! Naved, don't act mendacious, just tell me what you did to yourself."

It was not easy for him to tell her the truth.

But...

"Well, I made a vain attempt to hack the vein of my wrist."

Naved had to say this and Vedana began to cry her eyes out.

"Why did you do this, Naved?"

He replied quietness.

"There is my dad on the one side and you on the other. What do I do now? How should I conciliate my dad? Please don't do that ever after. I'll never leave you, I love you Naved............. I love you. Tell me, you'll take care of yourself. We'll just elope and marry in the court. But swear you don't repeat that nonsense, I don't want to lose you."

They talked and talked for long, not realising when they had gone off to sleep. In this way the more Vedana tried to widen the gap between the two, the opposite happened. Next morning she woke up with her eyes swollen and her face down.

When Pandit ji noticed it, he inquired, “Are you alright?”

“Ya dad, I’m .... I was studying late.”

All her daring that she acquired lying on the bed all night long, just dried up whenever her dad came before her. Now she had learned well that there was no way out but to hurry. But there was nobody at home to hear her out. Naved, on the other side was losing his trust in her little by little.

“Now you can ask me to leave anytime. Do you remember the promises of love that we made? It would be cheating on your part if you go ahead with someone else who will not be in the know that you were so close to someone in the past; and Almighty also knows this. I’m afraid lest He should trouble you ever for this socially approved adultery. But it’s alright if you’ve decided; I’ll see to my life myself, there’s nobody for me. Even my soul wants to quit me and now she can leave me alone anytime in the scorching heat of life, I cannot make it out how would be the day with you not around. How many breaths will be spared from that day onwards? You care about your life now. I’ll pray that it passes well, and that you don’t see any pain ever in your life. It doesn’t matter; in fact my luck is like this, I’ll be happy in your happiness............. Go, wherever you want to.”

"It's you who make me happy, and I'm not going anywhere," she put in.

"Please believe me, just forgive me once; I promise I won't leave you ever and will do whatever you say. Please you just plan something to find out a way, I can't survive without you, don't break my heart. Let's work out some solution, I won't do anything now on my own, I'll follow what you suggest." This way she tried to win his trust again.

"Just don't say please again and again. Let me sort it out but promise that you will always be with me."

"Of course, do something fast."

"Yeah, I will."

At this they ended the call.

Naved was under pressure about what to do and what not. While lost in cogitation, an idea reflected in his mind and he rang up Vedana at 1 o'clock in the night.

"If I do something, will you be with me?" he asked straight away.

A phone at midnight got Vedana astounded.

"I've promised you," said she in a semi-sleepy voice, "I'll do what you say, now tell me if you've found a way out."

"Nothing special, I just want to ask if you can meet me tomorrow."

"Why not? I will. But what's the plan?"

"Nothing, you just come over first and I'll tell you. And don't make me excuses. Make sure you reach there at 9 o'clock in the morning at Sharma's shop. I'll be waiting for you. OK, bye.......Night."

And he put the phone down without lending ear to the other side. Next morning Vedana set out at 9 o'clock in the morning for Sharma's and got there by half an hour. Naved was already there waiting for her with a friend.

"Hello!" she greeted and sat down.

"We won't sit here for long. You've to go with me to the mosque. We're going to do *Nikah* (marriage) today."

What Naved just said took her breath away.

"No," she voiced with bated breath.

"That's not the way we marry," she added squaring herself.

"But you promised me, you would do what I say," spoke he fretfully.

"Nobody at home knows anything and yikes, we're going to do it right away!"

"It means we're running away to get married. No, Naved ....please try to understand me. We can't do that. My parents will die of shame. I will get them to meet our wishes as soon as possible. Please give me some time," she reasoned adjusting herself.

She took exception to the proposal.

Her words moved his confidence.

"Listen sweetheart, I do not want to give you any pain. Why do you think so? Why don't you trust me ever? I'm so fateful that my soul-mate speaks her mind before I'm done," he expressed with his face blue.

"I'm rueful, I goofed! I didn't listen to you in full."

"Shall I resume? Let me finish, then we'll go to the mosque first, do *Nikah* there and then to the court and get our marriage registered there. Then you'll go to your home and I will go to mine. This will at least secure me and your parents won't force you."

"Is it plausible?"

"Yes! We'll have to do this. We'll leave for the mosque now. We have to finish things off by 3 or 4 o'clock in the evening. I've called my friends, a camera will be there and I've already informed a *Maulvi*. This is Mr Nawab, the litigator sitting here with me. In the mosque they will ask you your date of birth. Tell them as it is there in your high school marksheet, and provide me with your high school marksheet by tomorrow it will be required in the court for your age-proof. Happy now?" Naved explained his elaborate plot to her.

"Naved, I'm frightened."

It was nerve-racking for her.

"Oh! Come on dearie, don't you believe me? Now come on, hurry up! Or we'll be late."

She stood up as if with broken knees and moved ahead hand in hand with him. The couple made their way straight to the mosque where a *Maulvi* made her take a decisive step into Islam followed by all the rites and rituals as per Naved's plan. She got free at about 4:30 in the evening and straight reached home. She was not Vedana now she was Arshi alias Vedana. Things changed swiftly.

13

The Impasse

Rajeev was unknowingly coming within striking distance of Sabiha with every word they had between them. His and Rashmi's family being unaware of this were busy making preparations for their upcoming marriage. He'd begun to meet Sabiha too. She called it 'an unnamed relation' and denounced it as they were not bound to marry. Rajeev never cared of it; his phone usually remained busy at night.

Rashmi observed the change in him and his busy phone at odd hours obliged her to think otherwise. Once when she asked, he tried to cover it up by telling cock and bull stories.

Something devastating was happening in his mind; his marriage was fixed in the month of May but he got it postponed to November. He was in constant touch with Sabiha. She had changed a lot, she displayed maturity in her talk, and time had made her strong. She unceasingly reminded him of the fact that they could never be united. It was zero time for him; he was on the fork of road, unable to choose which way to go along-good for two or good for all.

At an ill-timed night he got a message from Rashmi while he was busy with sexting Sabiha; he was replying Sabiha but he miss-sent one to Rashmi. Though in no time he realised his inadvertence, he put everything to avert it from going to Rashmi; he did all possible tricks even switching off his cell phone. But what was ordained had to happen. It was 11:30 pm and Rashmi took no time to have a handle on it; she called back and without listening to him cited her decision.

She said, "I'm in the sure-know that you're going parallel with someone else and there is no chance of your coming back. I'm quite au-fait with the people in love as my elder sister's marriage is a love marriage. You might feign to get closer to me. But this is a lovers' skin saving fashion that they tell lies frequently and that is skin deep efficacious on me. And yes.............. I'll not denigrate you, I'll recant on my behalf, I won't say anything. You won't face any trouble. Have a good life ahead, Mr Rajeev!" saying so she disconnected the phone and turned that off altogether.

Rajeev called back but got the 'switched off' message, he didn't redial. He didn't do any other message to Sabiha and slept. Next morning he didn't go to the clinic with his father.

At 2 o'clock his father telephoned at home and spoke to his mother,

"Rashmi's father has spurned to move on with this relationship."

When Rajeev heard this, he was shaken inside for a while however Rashmi was a beautiful and decent girl. But now he couldn't do anything because he knew the reason and his father also denied to talk to anybody anymore. Rajeev's mother dared hard to tell this to him thinking it to be a thunderbolt for the boy. She informed Rajeev all about this; she was afraid if he'd be sad.

But he very plainly asked, "Why haven't they disclosed any reason?"

Rajeev already had this idea. On hearing this, he became twitchy, he felt as if he had lost something of a great worth and found himself hanging in the balance. His father was gloomy when he came back home in the evening. Seeing his father's funeral face, he turned more anxious for he had lost everything for nothing. Now he missed Rashmi more than Sabiha. He boozed uncontrollably that night.

Sabiha's uncle brought a very good proposal; the boy was an IPS officer. Without speaking to Sabiha, he had consented for it. He directed Amanullah to further the matrimonial matters.

Dr Amanullah informed his daughter,

"On Sunday they are visiting us."

She did not say anything but okay,

"What will I see? I'm after you."

It'd been five days since Rajeev broke up with Rashmi. He did not like it anywhere. Sabiha tried to call him up twice but he did not answer the phone. He hadn't recuperated fully from the road hold up and now this episode of tragedy devastated him badly. He was depressed. Everybody was vexed at his deteriorating health. The parents were eager to know what'd happened to him but he did not answer. Sabiha's marriage was fixed with the IPS officer. Rajeev stopped making or receiving Sabiha's phone calls. He went to the clinic on the very odd occasions.

One day he left home without informing anybody. He was so down in the dumps that he decided to kill himself. He directly went to a medical store and bought *Lonazet* tablets with those pills he reached the station and over there he gulped five of the pills and sat to wait for the train. Inside of five minutes the medicines took over him with their soporific effect and he lied down in the same place.

He had left his mobile and gold accessories at home when he left at eight thirty in the morning. Now it was 10 o'clock in the night. Dr Chander Kumar and his friends had rummaged for him everywhere in the city and ad extremum they informed the Police. The men in khaki, showing promptness, discovered him lying somnolent at the Meerut railway station at two the next day morning. Investigative officer had a doubt that he had taken some intoxicating drugs. He informed his father and took him to the civil hospital for a check-up, and he was kept there till he regained conscience.

His medical report showed overdose of sleeping pills. He woke up the next day in the evening and it made his family and well wishers have a sigh of relief. Completing other formalities they took him home. At home he wept his heart out embracing his mother and made a promise to her that he would never repeat anything like this ever in future. In the next few days he became normal.

Stoic Rajeev forgot both Sabiha and Rashmi and remembered only one—his mother.............!

14

Interblast Match

After a few days one more proposal came for Vedana. This time the boy was smart and their horoscopes too matched. Both of her younger brothers too cottoned to the boy very much. She had made up her mind to overcome the toughest ordeal in her life. This time she had no fortuity to decline the match.

Naved there went to the court almost each day to get the registration of their marriage in which he was eventually successful. He was carefree now as their marriage had been executed and legally he was now Vedana's husband and so Pandit ji couldn't marry his daughter anywhere else. He gave a photocopy of registration to Vedana and explained to her that she would show it at home whenever she'd be given excessive pressure and not to fear anymore.

"Request your parents that you can't live sans me and that we have also married. They will have to accept this, and if they don't, the law will take over. We don't need to fear anymore now. I'll seek for the consent of my parents too."

These were the pep-talks Naved gave her from time to time. He loved her very much and didn't want to lose her at any cost. She, on the other side felt difficult to pass every single day as her dad asked her daily when they should invite the boy's family home for the ritual of *Roka.* The boy's parents were telephoning them repeatedly and they wanted to know what to do next. As the boy was everyone's choice so everybody at home craved to get through with this auspicious job as quick as possible. She had already crossed 25 years of age and Pandit ji was under increasing social obligation to get his daughter married off.

"Shall I call them or not?" Pandit ji lashed out.

"Of course, dad, inform them to come over on May 7," said she.

"Listen daughter! I wish I could keep you always before my eyes but there are some social compulsions; daughters have to go to a new home one day."

Pandit ji was very pleased; he didn't take time to fix May 7 for inviting Deepak Bhardwaj and family. Both the families were on cloud nine with their new association and it reflected whenever they talked together. Preparations were going on there at Vedana's house to welcome their going-to-be family members. Her younger brothers were as pleased as Punch with their soon-to-be brother-in-law, who's up to their likes. While the whole family kept its spirits up, she saw her dreams fading away and her happiness dying. In this confusion the date of the *Roka* got closer. She realised it was high time she must unravel everything before her family or her parents would undergo great insult, and there would be problem at the time of marriages of her sibs. So she psyched herself up to unveil everything to her parents by April 30. Well, April thirty too calendared up and her courage gave up again; she was in fits all day long on April thirty about what to say and how?

In the evening, Pandit ji arrived home. He was not feeling well so he made it earlier that day. She was breathing hard to unburden her heart and looking for a psychological moment and as she beheld her dad coming in, she got into her mom's room and declared straight away,

"I can't marry there."

"Where?????!!!" asked mom with her mouth gaped.

"I'm talking about Deepak Bhardwaj," articulated she.

"What happened?? Have you driven yourself up the wall?" asked *Panditain*.

"Yes! I have," Vedana didn't contain it any longer.

"I won't marry there and I won't marry anywhere. If I think of marrying someone on this side of the grave, it would be Naved only."

What she just said made her mom's heart skip a beat and got on brothers' nerves,

"So you're still with him."

"Yes! I'm and I will always be till my last breath."

"This damsel is going to bring our nose down in society; she will leave us in the middle of nowhere. Where has this blood-sucker come from to ruin our family?"

And she towed her to Pandit ji's room.

"Just see what your dear daughter is saying?"

"Dad, I won't marry anyone except Naved, nobody at all," she shrilled.

"Just phone them right away and say 'No'. Nobody is coming around on the seventh; I'm not going to marry anyone. Never! Never! Naved! Only Naved!"

She burst out her heart.

Pandit ji felt helpless at that sudden and uncalled for shift.

"Vimla, inform them not to come and tell them that she doesn't like the boy. I can't do anything now. And ask her to go wherever she wants to; she is no more my daughter now. Let me sleep I'm feeling out of sorts," and Pandit ji showed them the way out and bolted his room.

"How far have you gone with him? What have you two been rendering? Why you are not able to forget him? You are set to ruin our family."

"I can't lose remembrance of him, mom, because I dote on him; he's my soul and if my soul leaves me this body made of five elements will fall down. Please just listen to me, I want your help. Let me live my life like this or snatch it away; but I won't go with somebody else. Not at any time!"

And that night was really dark for Pandit ji's family.

Next morning Pandit ji woke up with great difficulty; he had made up his mind to quit the job. He was downhearted and feeling lonely. Both of her brothers left for their work. Nakul, the elder one had joined a property dealer after passing intermediate due to the not-so-good financial conditions of the familial set-up and the second one, doing his twelfth grade, was good at studies and frequented school daily. In their absence Pandit ji talked to Vedana and his wife.

"My daughter knows that her dad is poor and can't procure a match as per her wish, so she kept him aside and took a decision about her life herself," he mumbled with his face down.

"All right, but............ an Allah maniac??? What in the world would the society say? That Pandit ji has got a Muslim son-in-law. How could I hear that? Is there any way out, Vedana, to come back?"

Vedana, who was standing nearby leaning on a box with her face hanging down, moved her head in negation,

"No dad! There's no way out for me too. I adore him and I'm going to marry him only for love or money; he's a very good boy, dad. Please don't force me..............." she burst out and went to her room.

Pandit ji was non-expectant with her response; he was so troubled that he lost all his hunger and thirst. He told *Panditain* that he had some important work and left; though she consented half-heartedly. After nearly ten hours at day-out, he came back home with Professor Goyal, the brothers too were at home. Professor Goyal took a seat and convoked Vedana who was out of hand.

"Daughter, how much do you respect me I don't know?" he said as Vedana turned up there, "but your dad takes me as his elder brother and venerates me a lot. I know him since you children were not even aware of your whereabouts; your dad has toiled hard to run and maintain this house, he quit his studies early and joined this clinic and has been working there still, just to brighten the future of you children, he kept his youth and his old age on parallels. He has never made any savings for his own old age just to carry on with your studies."

"*Bhabhiji,* you kindly go to some other room with the boys," Professor Sahib directed the *Panditain.*

"No, I won't," countered Nakul.

Professor Sahib at first didn't want him to be there but after a moment of reflection he agreed.

"Is this true what I've been told of?" he shot at Vedana.

She raised her eyelids heavily and surveyed her dad. Her goggle-eyes questioned something as if she had some inkling.

"Yes uncle! All that you heard is true," she fessed up looking at her dad.

"Why did you do that, sweetie? What did you see in him? The biggest predicament is that he is Muslim, an heir of Mohd Gori while we are Hindu, descendents of Prithvi Raj Chauhan," Professor Sahib asked.

"Just look at me, Vedana. I'm like your father and so just pay heed to what I say. There's nothing called love; there can be no love between a Multi-God worshiper and a Mono-God supporter. These damn Muslim boys keep Hindu names and trap ingenuous Hindu girls and make them Muslim, this all is part of what they call love-*jihad*, an invitation to Islam. Their stories are void of even one iota of truth. Believe me! You are a well educated girl and so consecrated how you did get caught into their snare? I'm unideaed and clueless to see that. ....," enticed he.

"Speak something, Vedana!" advanced Goyal Sahib with these therapeutic sentences.

"Uncle, he and his family may be the meanest people of the world. They could be terrorists; and doing *jihad* but I'm bound to marry him or not live without him. These intolerant accusations are neither here nor there and not enough to divert my course of love. Nothing can change my mind now, I'm hell bent on going ahead with this relationship..... I think the world of Naved ....And listen uncle, all the shit you talk about-caste and community, high and low, good and bad, *jihad* and *teerth* ....Humans have made them and not God. God's made all humans alike," she cried out and turned to go to her room.

"What the murky are you saying? Don't you remember how Pakistanis behead many of our soldiers and kill our innocent people in their gaols so brutally?"

"Pakistanis and Indian Muslims are not synonyms rather they are apples and oranges. It's poor haveral Hindus' predicament that they can not distinguish between these two."

"Don't preach, missy, your wisdom seems to have been consumed; you may think that they are not one but we beg to differ. Just sit here and listen to the uncle and listen with rigour, you can't shout us down," cautioned Nakul grabbing her hand tightly.

"He's right because it's only Hindu girls who get into the baited trap. About one year ago one of my friends fell in love with a girl who was Muslim but when her brothers knew this they threatened to butcher him and got him away from her. And within days they brought out her marriage. What's happening to you? I've seen both. Deepak is much ahead of Naved in all aspects. You're bound to follow us or there are other ways too," iracund Nakul bawled furiously the first time and left all aghast.

She jolted her hand free and vamoosed inside; she was not ready to hear of anyone.

He ran after her.

"Numskull, don't throw tantrums; you can't put the rest of us out of your way just for your self-indulgence. Just open up your mind and quit this damning doggedness. Control yourself bolshy dolt or you will leave us not worthy of showing our face in society," Nakul continued.

"No! No! Nothing can be done now. I've got Hobson's choice, either Naved or death. I'm your daughter and you can choose either. I won't say anything," declared Vedana haughtily.

"Jongo jenny, don't be so stubborn, or we have another option too and that is to send your beau away from this world. I'll live the rest of my life behind the bars but I can't see that my family lives a life of abuse. I'm going right away to put him to death. What happens will be seen later," raged Nakul.

He had hardly finished when everybody jumped over him and clutched him tight.

"Just unhand me, uncle; this girl has made our life troublesome. It's been one year that we're observing change in her. She no more belongs to our family now. Let me go! I'll kill that wud bastard," he yelled so and so that Vedana moved to fetch her registration of marriage.

"Go and make me widow," she sniveled throwing it on her brother's face.

"Go and do that and I won't have another marriage."

The moment the piece of paper flew, the din fell silent. Professor Sahib grabbed at the paper and wore his pair of spectacles to peruse, when he went through it, he got his eyes hoisted because the paper read that Vedana had changed her faith and married Naved four months ago.

"Oh gosh! Oh gosh!!! Shit............," breathed Professor Sahib sitting on a sofa. "What the juvenility has she done, without giving you a single cue? She's really going to render blood letting............ Everyone, be seated please," spoke miffed Professor Sahib defeatedly.

Panditain was shedding tears at a stretch. The scene touched the brothers too, "Dad, I got to do something now."

"No son!" Pandit ji tried to hold him up.

"Vedana, is this the pay off for all my sacrifice that I made just for you children and this is the compensation for that?" Pandit ji was nearing collapsing.

Professor Sahib caught his hand and took him out on the gate, "Just take care of yourself and don't be so tense. I'll leave for now with this paper but I'll be back by the sun-down. Try to calm down things at home. Don't wash your dirty linen in public, I'll fine tune everything. Believe me," said Professor Sahib sagaciously.

"My knees are broken now. It's you who can do something about this; whatever may be the perception but it is only because of you people's shrill whistling that the community slumbers peacefully," said Pandit ji breaking into torment, "She is no more anyone to me."

"Now this is not an issue of the family but that of our community at large. We're not being able to keep our sisters and daughters safe within our country. Forget about Rinkal Kumari of another country, Rinkals are unsafe in India too. I damn Hindus, I damn Hindusthan. I'll be back by the formation of the twilight arch and till the time you don't worry at all."

Professor Sahib met up lots of people all day long and went to his friends who were lawyers too but no way. Ultimately a black coat clad suggested him that divorce was the only solution to terminate the relationship and no other solution existed; but that was possible only after the consent of both the parties.

"Will they take divorce? They won't ever hear about that," doubted Professor Sahib.

Even then he pondered on the suggestion and telephoned Pandit ji. He picked up the phone, "How are things at home now?" Professor Sahib asked, "Mind, you don't let her go out or sit alone furtively."

"She is having a siesta after eating a little," said her father.

"So I should not be there now; but I inform you that this paper is the registration of marriage in the court and this is genuine. The only solution to this problem is that they both divorce willingly. She's now Naved's other half on legal grounds. For divorce you'll need to talk to Dr Amanullah, so just call him out. If you see him at home, this will add to complication only, so better you call him to my home," Goyal Sahib suggested.

And this way the holy bond of love was going to be sacrificed at the altar of communal insanity. The two who had to live together for lives were being parted before they could unite.

Pandit ji made a bold step and called up Dr Amanullah. He recounted each and every thing to him. When he had finished talking, Doctor Sahib got almost faint-hearted; he hardly believed his ears as to what had happened. He retook the same words,

"What the heck have the children done?"

"Please save me from this shame," Pandit ji wore mourning.

"I'm just coming to your house at the top of Usain Bolt's speed; I will close the clinic right now. Don't lose heart, everything will be fine."

Dr Aman shut down the clinic and reached Pandit ji's place, where the latter received him at the gate and out off hand took him for a rendezvous. He showed Doctor Sahib the piece of paper and apprised him how the children had committed fiasco.

It took Dr Amanullah unawares.

"You tell us Professor Sahib what can be done to dilute this icy-solid and formidable difficulty?" asked Naved's father in a shrieking voice.

"See Doctor Sahib, this thin piece of paper is the certificate of court-marriage and it declares them to be legal man and wife, now there is only one solution to terminate this legal relation and that is divorce and that too in a legal way at the court and execution of which requires the yielding of both Naved and Vedana. You get your son to do it and we will get our daughter. And the sooner the better it would be for us because you know how marriage between a Muslim boy and Hindu girl is looked upon in India. This is not Pakistan where Hindu girls are forced to convert their faith. But this doesn't happen here, Doctor Sahib, you are like my brother and I hope you act the same way."

"Bhai Sahib, I'm still feeling unstable on my feet. I will go home and take expose of everything from Naved and then meet you at my earliest," said he.

"See Bhai Sahib, it is Vedana's betrothment on the seventh of May; and it is already the second today, everything is out in the open now. This paper tells us everything; just put the matter across to him here at my house. Meanwhile I will arrange for the divorce papers; remember this is the question of Pandit ji's reputation together with his life, so please make it fast."

"Sure, I understand, so I'll be here tomorrow with my son. And Naved is your son too so I look forward to your help also in making him understand the subtlety of the matter."

"I'll leave now, see you tomorrow."

"And Pandit ji, you haven't come for two days?" continued Doctor Sahib.

"My daughter has not made me eligible to go anywhere in the society."

"Please don't say that, everything will be okay, *Inshallah*. We are all with you and will adopt a feasible expedient to bring you out of this delicate matter. Don't keep your spirits down," sympathised Doctor Sahib.

"I had better leave now, *Khuda Hafiz*."

Doctor Sahib reached home, where he discussed about it with his wife and Naved. When he asked Naved he affirmed everything to be true and made it clear that he had two options-only Vedana or death. Doctor Sahib cajoled him to agree to break up the relationship but he didn't change his mind and when he told him that they would be going to Pandit ji's house the next morning, he refused.

"Dad, you are also with them," said Naved with his eyes filled with tears.

"This is the toughest time of my life, please be with me................ I'm your son."

"I'm with you but escaping from the circumstances won't do, you have to face it and so you are going with me tomorrow. What to do further we will discuss over there. By the way you want my support today but did you ever bother to inform me about what was going on? And yes, everything is not in my hands; there will be several people who will take decision as per the communal red tape. I'm calling your uncle Sadiqullah inasmuch as he is the numero uno of our family, he'll accompany us or I alone wouldn't be able to say anything among so many polytheists," cleared Doctor Sahib.

It was a stroke of luck upon him to see his fiduciary love-relation become public; not only he but no one ate anything.

Doctor Sahib passed through the night shaking and breaking in anxiety and fear and very hardly managed to catch on some sleep. Again the same dream flashed through his mind recalling which would always shake his heart and soul. He saw the same old man with open arms muttering something distressingly. As if to say "Don't go with them, son........... Please don't go..........Come back..........We are waiting for you..........Come back home, son..........Please don't leave your father alone.......... Don't fear them........... Don't turn back to your family.

A series of gruesome scenes followed and began to run in his mind. One time he saw himself and that old man amidst a huge gathering of Hindu saints and *Sanyasis* rallied together at some Hindu pilgrimage, when suddenly a malicious cavalry of Turkish assailants with waving swords and spears raided them and started savagely massacring them. The other moment he saw hills of Hindu skulls with a skull-face of the old man lying within.

And all of a sudden his uncontrollably racing heart and pounding head threw him out of the nightmare into reality.

That night was one of the scariest nights for him which he spent breathing hard.

Anyway the morning came and he called up Pandit ji,

"My brother, Naved and me, we tripartite are coming, at around 11 o'clock we will make it to professor Goyal's residence," Doctor Sahib informed Pandit ji and put the phone down.

Then he telephoned his elder brother Hadji Sadiqullah and gave him the superficial account. Hadji Sahib didn't speak much on the phone but remarked tactfully,

"It takes two to clap."

"*Bhaijaan,* it is 8:30 now, you just make it quick and be here as soon as possible," reminded the younger one.

"Yeah, I'll leave shortly, just let me have my breakfast as I've to take medication. You just wait, I will reach there," said the elderly linchpin.

Anyway he got at younger's by 9 o'clock and spent two hours there, took blow-by-blow account from his brother and then set out to see Pandit ji. They reached Professor Sahib's bhavan at 11:30 am in Hadji's jalopy, where they found Professor Sahib and Pandit ji waiting for them. They had Naved along with them.

Professor Sahib himself went to the door and led them to the living room. Everybody took seats and came to the bottom line without a hold up-discussion about Naved and Vedana's kismet, nothing else.

There was a strange silence in the air.

"Doctor Sahib, did you have a word with your son?" Professor Sahib broke the ice.

"Why don't you ask him?' Doctor Sahib replied.

"OK son, you speak what happened?" put Professor Sahib.

"Sir, I love Vedana very much. Can I not wive her?" questioned Naved plainly.

"Listen son, there are things that we call community, society, religion etc., if we go against them it wouldn't do us good", Professor Sahib explained amicably.

"But sir……… every faith, every community, every guru, every God and even human-all of them enlighten us to live with love. I didn't see her religion, caste or something when I fell in love with her, it just happened, and we are through with marriage too and it's only for the sake of uncle that I didn't take her away with me covertly. What I wanted was uncle and auntie's consent to fix our marriage and do it socially."

"But son if this unison were that easy and social, I myself would move ahead and get it effected. Have you ever seen an inter-faith marriage that you are talking about? And in our society this is de trop. In yesterday's newspaper a father garroted his daughter inasmuch as she loved a Hindu boy while they were Muslims."

"It's easy to quote things like that but if something really happens like that Pandit ji will die an easy death, the family will be ruined and nothing will be left. Apply yourself, my child, don't be out of mind, you're mature, smart and hailing from a good and generous background, well educated too; please try to feel pain of others!"

……………………*PAUSE*………………………..

"So just sign the papers for a divorce."

"If it's so Professor Sahib then you call your daughter too, let's delve deep into the matter because a divorce requires the consent of both," Hadji Sadiqullah butted in.

"No! No, Hadji Sahib we'll solve it on our daughter's behalf so she won't come. It's enough of affront already, you just get Naved to sign the papers," Professor Sahib brushed aside.

"I can't stay here anymore, I won't sign, I would rather kick the bucket," screamed Naved.

"One minute, one minute... stop Naved! Don't take leave of your senses; keep your wits about yourself and just sit here," Hadji Sahib sprang up to grab Naved and made him sit.

"Professor Sahib, it's the hot blood, in seconds they will do something destructive and will leave us nowhere; you just listen to what I say and get Vedana here. Kindly feel the pulse of the matter, I beseech you."

"Yes Pandit ji, do you agree?" Prof Sahib put forth.

"Just give it a thought and do what you think is right. OK! I'll go myself and get her; you all please sit, gentlemen......... and wait for ten minutes. Just have tea and snacks. Sachin, bhai, arrange for some tea and snacks, we have got guests over here."

Professor Sahib was used to calling his wife this way inasmuch as his only son Sachin Mittal was an engineer and lived in France and by doing so he felt his son's presence always around and found aesthetic pleasure.

Saying so he left to call Vedana and in ten minutes he was back with her; Pandit ji felt uncanny and dishonored as if being butchered socially on a traffic circle, yet he kept silent and observed whatever came off. Vedana came and sat beside her dad.

"Daughter, for the sake of several people here, please form the conclusion of this relationship" Professor Sahib initiated.

She uttered nothing.

"Do you really want to break up, Vedana?" Naved took lead.

She moved her head heavily in refusal.

"My child," Sadiqullah Sahib got a word in edgeways, "this relation is not acceptable as Islam doesn't allow marrying a Non-Muslim person, so break it up yourself and you can save two families from crashing down; and Naved, you please just beef up your heart, son!"

"I can't uncle, I can't...," he sounded off.

"If I separate my soul from my body I would not survive. Please don't say that, I'm not short of anything-above all I have intellect. I'll always keep her cheerful as I love her more than anything. What the hell in this caste and community for the sake of which you people want to disunite two lovers? Professor Sahib wants a Hindu groom and you uncle, you want a Muslim bride; you both have to do nothing with the beatitude of your son or daughter. Isn't it? See then, I declare myself to be Hindu and from today on my name is Naved Sharma. And Vedana................ You become Muslim and your name is Arshi Khan."

Peculiar silence prevailed for a while.

"Are you glad now? Now let us live, now I can be the son-in-law of Pandit ji because I'm a Hindu-Brahmin and Vedana your daughter-in-law, uncle because she's a Muslim now and nobody will come between us because the next way out is suicide only. You guys should be contented now."

Naved screamed with his heart burning, he scurried out of the room and left everybody there awe-stricken. A queer silence shrouded the place again.

He left them with nothing to speak. Everyone was speechless; silence just surrounded them and he appeared again in two three minutes.

"What's the issue now? You've got a Pandit son-in-law and you've got a Muslim daughter-in-law, uncle. Now let's leave and live."

"No Sonnie! You're talking abstract and that doesn't mean anything," Professor Sahib breaks the congealed atmosphere.

"You'll have to go to the temple and worship there."

"What are you saying Professor Sahib?" Sadiqullah Sahib checked in.

"The boy has already gone insane; you're showing signs too, you seem to be getting out of your mind. You are not on the right side of sixty five, so act your age. We should leave forthwith, we can't do anything now."

"Naved, make a move."

"No uncle, I won't go," rebuffed he.

"Okay, let's get up and move, Aman. Naved is no more our son. Let them go wherever their destiny leads them to; there is nothing in our hands. Stand up Aman, let's go home, the children have gone so far that they can't be brought back now, it would be better to leave them to their own devices."

Anyhow both of the brothers clutched the hand of Naved and marched off. En route for home, he visited a newspaper office.

At night he locked himself in his room and the following day he got up at eight and left the house saying that he would be back soon.

The very next day Naved gave the declaration in the newspaper that he now would be known as Naved Sharma and his wife Vedana, Arshi Khan. About 10 o'clock he reached Vedana's house. He had the newspaper in his hand and two policemen along with him; he met Pandit ji and her brothers and let them know that he had become Hindu showing the declaration in the newspaper. Naved beseeched them to let Vedana go with him but her brothers didn't bear it and in a fit of choler they hit him before the cops, but legally he, after a slanging match with Nakul, succeeded in taking her with him.

"Daughter, don't go. I was over elated to have a female child at the time of your birth though relatives opposed. I said to the world that my daughter would make me feel proud someday, I didn't know you'd requite me for my love like this. Where are you going??? Don't you bear in mind those childhood piggyback rides? The onus is on you to save my life."

"Have a heart!" begged Pandit ji when she turned her back at him.

It was so sensitive and appalling that Pandit ji's final words fell on her deaf ears, all his entreaties appeared hollow to her that had left her cold; he was left lamenting severely and her brothers burning in rage as cops didn't let anything unpleasant happen.

Ultimately Vedana left her family in anguish following the same age old trail on which millions of Hindus were forcibly compelled to leave their home.

Vedana's parting like this afflicted Pandit ji's family badly. It was very hard rather impossible for Pandit ji to tolerate the ungainly episode, and after ten days a severe cardiac arrest took him away.

15

Kaka's Agitation

In the same time a great Gandhian and a social reformer Kaka Sahay's movement against corruption had reached the pinnacle. Kaka had observed many fasts to compel the Government to pass a strong anti-corruption bill in the parliament. The Government was helpless. It didn't have any feasible formulae to curb the corruption and inflation. The party in power was without any options as it's their own leaders who were corrupt. The politically acrimonious statements of the opposition about the party in power were worsening the aura more. It was not so that they were allowed for corrupt practices; they were isolated in their own party.

This is the Indian political model in which corrupts can win sitting in jails. These corruptors ask for votes in the name of some good leaders of their party and go ahead by saying that they have been snared in a conspiracy of the rivals or the opposition, and the veil of the word 'conspiracy' keeps their misdoings entombed.

Moreover they compare themselves with Bhagat Singh, Azad and many more by saying,

"They were also put behind bars."

The helpless government too did not have any other option but to bring forth inflation. Petrol was Rs 100 per liter and milk Rs 80 per liter as it was under pressure of development, for that it needed money. Big scams of lacs and crores had stirred the Government very sternly. The Government had multiple problems-big scams of its leaders, pressure of development and the Kaka factor and so on.

Kaka's effect was obvious now. Though people didn't have time to gather in the maidans yet they had set their minds for a big political crusade. Ruling party was losing its public support. Being dazzled by this, the Government made headway by putting crusaders in gaols on wrongfully coined charges.

Roots of corruption are so deep in our country that everybody is affected by this in one way or the other.

Though dissident Kaka alone was enough for eradicating corruption but he was very dark that his people had been trapped and jailed.

Rajeev's doctor had diagnosed his headache as a Brain Tumor which was in critical stage. Due to which he was unable to work, he stopped going to the clinic. He kept himself confined to his room. His treatment was going on under Dr Yash Sawhney (a famous neurologist). For treatment he used to go Delhi. During one of his doctor visits, he got to know that Kaka was on fast in Delhi. It was the first day of his fast and the Government was not even least bothered about it.

At this Rajeev thought of joining Kaka's fast as he did not want to waste his life. He determined to do something remarkable and salutary for the nation. Losing such a precious life for nothing or for a girl is a mean act, so he joined Kaka's fast till death; he decided to lay down his life pluckily for the great cause of national and social welfare.

The Government got fumed at seeing a young doctor with Kaka on fast. With him he raised one more issue of child-raping that had been stirring the nation for last half a decade. Rape of girl children had been in trend for last several years more vividly. A crime that was growing into an epidemic and people were scared of bringing up their children in such a horrible atmosphere.

On the twenty first day of fast when Kaka was in the ICU, the Government bowed to Rajeev and passed the anti-corruption bill in the Loksabha. The bill recommended death sentence for the corruptors and more specifically for the paedophiles and the rapists of any age. Rajeev became famous as Junior Kaka. He neither married nor went back home ever, for the rest of his life he continued to fight for the welfare of the nation and the society.

And last year he martyred himself in the Ramleela Maidan, New Delhi while observing fast till death demanding the Government to pass an ordinance to curb the population explosion, but the entreaty fell on the deaf ears of the Government being led by the multi children demagogues.

On balance I would say 'being in love is good but with nation.

Dear reader, don't get confused with 'I'. I am Raghu Nandan Goyal, the younger brother of Professor V K Goyal and neighbour of Pt Bholaram and of course the narrator of the story. I got account of the story from my elder brother and the diaries of Vedana and Naved that I collected from the investigative officer in Vedana's murder case.

16

Vindicativeness

Nakul, the elder son was burning with rage and was unable to succumb to the family-disrepute. He vowed to be revenged on the couple. His life had changed drastically and now he shouldered his family, but that humiliation never left his head, he harboured a strong grudge against his sister and her lover. Obamamaniac Nakul'd intended to teach them a very harsh lesson and so contrived locating them to give shape to his idea.

When he tried to find the couple, he came to know that Naved hadn't gone to his house ever since he married; the same day he had left home for good with Vedana. Now it was difficult for Nakul to trace them but not impossible because both belonged to the same city and most friends of Naved were there in Meerut as well as those of Vedana too. He was so hurt that he abhorred the word 'love' for which his sister left all of them who really doted on her. He could not conclude if it was love or something else that she had sacrificed all for the one who was not worth. He was striving to trawl them with all his might.

After around three months he got to know that Naved was working in a company at Manesar and living in Gurgaon in a rented accommodation. As soon as he came to know this he set off to Gurgaon. On the internet he sieved the list of employees of the company and spidered web pages to gather data about him. Going hard with it he finally detected the exact address they were dwelling at. He went to Gurgaon to confirm his topographic findings.

With all the information, he came back to Meerut; he acquired a local gun from there and ran off to Gurgaon again. After two days he encountered the chance he had been waiting and for which he had gone there. It was Sunday, Naved and Vedana were moving to a temple on their motor scooter. Nakul put on helmet and dogged them hard on his bike. When they moved through a vacant street, Nakul sped up his bike and hit them down, and then he pulled his gun out and fired it blindly at them.

He whined in anger and rage, "It is enough now. Jodha Bai to Vedana and hundreds of years.........No, no, no..........Now no more Vedanas.........No more pain to any dejected Pandit ji.........No more destructive Nakul..........No more honour stains.........No more agitation of feelings......... er

..........No more injury to reputation......... No more social hounding.......... No more relentless religion conversion.........gak!"

Unfortunately Vedana got shot thrice but Naved escaped and wormed his way to the nearby house. He wanted to shoot Naved too but the gun didn't work. Though Naved got off the bullets, he got injured badly in his back. The sound of shooting a gun got the people around out of their homes.

Meanwhile, somebody called police too, choleric Nakul sank down whiningly. A Police Control Room van patrolling in nearby areas caught him on the spot with weapon.

They were rushed to the hospital where Vedana was declared brought dead because of over bleeding. She was in her gestation period. Naved was admitted to the ICU due to serious wounds and a few days later he was shifted to the general ward.

During the time no one came to see him or even bothered to take his news or his whereabouts, not even his friend Taufique who had been fuming at him on being Hindu. Vedana's sudden demise left Naved badly shattered. After around a month, he was discharged. He was now all alone in the world; his family had taken him to be in hell the day he declared himself to be Hindu. When he was in hospital he kept on buzzing...

Where have you gone, leaving me alone?
With you I was a blessed-life,
But now I am a heap of many a bone.
Why can't you see me mourn?
I'm waiting for you, lying prone.
Listen to my heart-cry, don't be deaf-stone.
Where have you gone, leaving me alone?

Where have you gone, leaving me alone?
Heart is brimming with so many things to share
And life is much too short to say,
Why you have unseemly kept yourself away?
Now my life is very short to home,
Why don't you come back to me alone?
Where have you gone, leaving me alone?

Where have you gone, leaving me alone?
I feel you always around me,
Your fragrance keeps me deep in you.
I can't think of anything but you
I don't pine for anything but you
You live in my eyes from dawn to dawn.
Where have you gone, leaving me alone?

Where have you gone, leaving me alone?
Whatever you like, you can say,
But there is nothing but love to stay.
O my soul, take up this fleshy mound
Your love finds it tough to live among hounds.
For any mistake, I did, I atone.

But tell me, tell me, tell me

Where have you gone, leaving me alone?
Where have you gone, leaving me alone?

……………………………………

……………………………………

In upshot of this foul play Vedana's youngest brother Vakul shifted to Delhi with his mother whereas Nakul was on trial for murder.

The suffering of losing Vedana took Naved into depression, he failed to deal with the vicissitudes– he quit his job, isolated himself from the world and even abandoned his devices of social connectivity. He wrote poems in memory of Vedana. He paid for the rent and food out of his savings; but how long would it suffice?

In three months when he ran out of money he vacated the house and started living rough at the railway station. Impecunious Naved was lost in the doldrums ever since Vedana died.

At the station, homeless, penniless or rather everything-less Naved composed a very touching poem:

I may not have a bricky palatial house
But I have soft eyelids to keep you in.
I may not have so much of paper money
But I have lots of love to spend all the way.

O my love, where have you gone away.
I may not have beautiful words for you to say
But I have a heart for you full of loveful pray.
Your absence is always ready to slay.
How will I live without you rest of the day?

O my love, why have you gone away?
I may not have much life left to play
But I have a heart, beats for you every moment, every day.
I may not have precious metals or stones to make you up.
But I have eyes that see you always beauteous.

O my love; please come back to your love!
....
....

One day one of the colleagues of his company happened to see him. He got goose bumps to find him in such a dreadful condition; he approached him to inquire about his piteous state.

"Naved, what has happened to you? All of a sudden you disappeared!"

"Bhai Ashutosh, there's nothing left for me now that I might live for, I'll pass all the time of my life left out this way or the other and then I'd be there where my Vedana is....................."

Ashu listened to his nonsense for some time but he soon felt that Naved had become duppie and was not normal at mind so he took him home. There he discussed it with his friends who rallied around him in order to take Naved to a rehabilitation centre with the help of an NGO. He began to recover there gradually. Lost in the memory of his lost love, poemsmith Naved coined:

Never do I say anything,
Never do I ask.
Tears are in my eyes,
And lonely is my heart,
You can neither see me moaning
Nor hear agonising groaning.
Like a blowing out wick,
I am lying lovesick.
Tides of questions arouse in me,
My eyes are crying for you to see,
But your decision is all above that
You'll never come back any further,
But I feel you always around.

Never do I say anything,
Never do I ask or laugh.
Tears are in my eyes
And pain in my heart.
I silently saw you going,
Did not disclose to anyone my lamenting.

Ohhh, my heart is pouring blood
.......my mind is pouring blood.
But all is going in vain as
Nobody is there to witness.
Pain is what I feel I say,
Perennial darkness's gripped nights and day.
In wish to see you, eyes've grown glazed.

Never do I say anything,
Never do I ask or laugh,
Tears are in my eyes
And pain in my heart.
....
....

By that time he had understood that everything be it home, family, religion or whatever, has to be abandoned for love. More's the pity, he did all renunciation, overcame all the Everests, yet he didn't win his love.

Through religion we only learn to live with love but we don't actually. After being better, the reincarnated Naved started revising people like him at the rehabilitation centre.

Jai Maa! Jai Hind!